CW01678079

info

# The complet

Distributed by:

UK
A.A. Publishing
(A Division of the
Automobile Association)
Fanum House
Basingstroke
Hampshire RG21 2EA

Australia
Gordon & Gotch Ltd,
25-37 Huntingdale Road,
Burwood
Victoria 3125

Tourist Publications

First published and produced
in Australia in 1990 by:

T.P. Books & Print Pty Ltd
Suite 13, 3 Moore Lane
Harbord Village
Harbord NSW 2096

In Association with:

Tourist Publications
6 Pilliou Street
Koliatsou Square
112 55 Athens, Greece



| | |
|---|---|
| Editorial Directors: | L. Starr<br>Y. Skordilis |
| Author: | Bill Howie |
| Typography: | M. Roetman |
| Design: | C. Mills |
| Layout: | C. Mills |
| Photosetting: | Deblaere Typesetting Pty Ltd |
| Photographs: | Japan Nat. Tourist Org. |
| Maps: | Judy Trim |

Printed in Australia

ISBN 1 872163 35 1



Due to the wealth of information available, it has been necessary to be selective. Sufficient detail is given to allow the visitor to make choices depending on personal taste, and the information has been carefully checked. However, errors creep in and changes will occur. We hope you will forgive the errors and omissions and find this book a helpful companion.

# ABOUT THIS GUIDE

Tokyo the enigma, Japan's capital, the administrative and political hearbeat of the nation, the city which set the pace for Japan's total social structure.

The plough has been replaced by the computer work space, the rice bowl by the McDonald's hamburger and the kimono by designer jeans. But underneath it all Japanese society remains a society with aggresive retention of traditional values and a culture yearning for the privacy of past decades.

This guide will help you to explore and appreciate the past and modern Japan, its Samurai history and its cultural superiority.

**Part I** gives general information on Japan and Tokyo, including history, culture, climate, geography, language and the day to day influence on Japanese life.

**Part II** takes you through Tokyo itself, the sights and sounds of the city and its environs. This section also brings you a brief but practical overview of Tokyo's main tourist attractions, what to do and what to see.

**Part III** consists of a full accommodation listing with useful additional information.

**Part IV** is the practical section, starting before you arrive and taking you through shopping and eating and a page or two for help!

**Part V** has been designed with the business visitors in mind but tourists will also find it very helpful.

You will need more than an itinery when you visit this land. Take your time and study the background, the people, the customs, the history. With the assistance of this guide book I hope that you will enjoy Tokyo and I am sure that you will find the experience both fascinating and rewarding.

# ACKNOWLEDGEMENTS

We gratefully acknowledge the assistance of **Japan Airlines**, **Takinawa Prince Hotel** and **JCT Wholesale Tours** in obtaining material. We especially thank **Helen Goodall** of **Japan Airlines**, Sydney and **Graham Copeland** of **Jaltour**, Melbourne for their efforts.

## Table of Contents

銀座駅
Ginza Sta.
銀座線
日比谷線
丸ノ内線
ミハラ

# PART I

## General Introduction

*Asakusa Kannon Temple*

# JAPAN AND HER PEOPLE

*'Japan does not disappoint the stranger; she corrects his fancies .... and then begins to enrich him with her truths.'*

Edmund Blunden, The Mind's Eye, 1934

Tokyo is not only Japan's capital, the administrative and political heartbeat of the nation, but she also sets the pace for Japan's total social structure. And yet, the country as a whole has the final say. As one gets to know the city, gradually it dawns, for all the sophistication and urban frenzy, Tokyo is really a collection of 'villages' where rural values still lurk, never far below the surface.

This is the enigma of Tokyo as the face of modern Japan and the secret of that enigma is to be found in the very framework of the social fabric.

High technology, Westernised values and an unabashed enthusiasm for capitalism are, all, merely the superficial face of a feudal society.

The plough has been replaced by the computer work space; the rice bowl by the McDonald's hamburger; the kimono by designer jeans. In other words, the final mixture has been updated but not necessarily the basic ingredients. Underneath the facade is still that conformity of a peasant society with its aggressive retention of traditional values and a cultural yearning for the privacy of those past decades when Japan turned in on herself and locked the doors to the outside world.

This explains the slave-like devotion of the workers to The Company; the complete obeisance to authority; the inability of foreigners to assimilate; the total lack of any foreign 'ghettos' the ingrained pride in the Samurai history; the cultural superiority that pays the barest respect to off-shore influences; and the self-effacing manner which can conceal a steely will.

Westerners living here tell of their frustration in knowing they will never be fully accepted into Japanese society: *once a foreigner, always a foreigner!* Like an atheist candidate for priesthood, the best one can do is to master the rites and learn the liturgy - there will be no ordination.

It justifies a range of behaviour from the complex rituals of doing business to the surprising rudeness of subway crowds (a resident will go to great pains to help a visitor baffled by the language and then cheerfully trample him under foot in the race for a seat).

To the tourist on a fleeting stopover to other ports, Tokyo appears black and white. The snap judgements are made and the city is instantly categorised. The shades of grey only come with time and repeated visits.

You will need more than an itinerary when you visit this land. Study its background, its people, its customs and its history.

The rewards are self evident.

## GEOLOGY AND GEOGRAPHY

Fanning out in an arc off the cost of the North East Asian mainland the islands of Japan are divided into the four major islands, **Hokkaido, Honshu, Shikoku** and **Kyushu**, and 3,000 minor islands. They extend from Latitude 25 degree North to Latitude 45 degree North. Looking at a map the southern tip of the main islands is roughly on a parallel with Shanghai below the Korean peninsula whilst the northern tip stretches off the far Eastern coast of the U.S.S.R. and is separated from the Soviet island of Sakhalin by a short width of the **Soya Sea.** In length they would exceed 3000 kms. whilst the total land area is 378,000 sq.kms.

The largest island is **Honshu** of 231,000 sq.kms. with 490 cities including the nation's six largest, **Tokyo, Yokohama, Osaka, Nagoya, Kyoto** and **Kobe.** 80% of the population live on Honshu.

*Honshu* (once known by the alternative name of Hondo) is about the size of Britain. The mountainous nature of the island has forced much of the population into corridors between the coast and the spine of mountains that dominate the central region.

Geologically Japan is part of the *'Ring of Fire'*, the circle of volcanic and earthquake activity which runs as a rim around the Pacific from the Americas through Japan and down to New Zealand. Tremors are frequent (more of nuisance value than dangerous), however the country is aware of the potential for destruction following the devastating earthquake of 1923 when tens of thousands perished in the 'quake and the subsequent fires. Tokyo must be one of the few cities, if not the only one, to have a special **Earthquake Memorial Museum** (see Part II). Although well aware of the situation and with contingency plans drawn up, the city authorities must dread the prospect of another major earthquake which would have catastrophic results due to the high population density, the extensive and crowded subway system and roads which would not be able to cope with any mass evacuation.

*Kodomono Shrine*

## CLIMATE

The 21 degrees of latitudinal difference in the Japanese islands means a range of climates from alpine to subtropical. This extends from the winter freezes in Hokkaido to the temperate balminess of Okinawa.

Honshu, and Tokyo in particular, is blessed with definite seasons: cool Autumns, chilly Winters, mild Springs and hot and humid Summers.

Summers and winters are affected by strong air patterns. In summer the monsoons bring the high humidity but in winter an eastward flow of dry, cold air from Siberia causes heavy snowfalls on the eastern side of the country.

The rains during the early part of summer are called the **Tsuyu**, an all purpose word meaning 'rainy season', 'dew' or 'soup'.

Spring is the best time to visit Tokyo before the humid summer days and the pollution set in. The climate is mild and pleasant and the flowering of the cherry blossoms (April/May) makes everything seem right with the world. October, as the country eases into Autumn, is also an easy time in which to travel.

Tokyo's monthly average temperatures (high and low):

| | | | | | |
|---|---|---|---|---|---|
| Jan: | 47°F | 8°C | Jul: | 84°F | 29°C |
| | 29 | -2 | | 70 | 21 |
| Feb: | 48°F | 9°C | Aug: | 86°F | 30°C |
| | 31 | -1 | | 72 | 22 |
| Mar: | 54°F | 12°C | Sep: | 79°F | 26°C |
| | 36 | 2 | | 66 | 19 |
| Apr: | 63°F | 17°C | Oct: | 69°F | 21°C |
| | 46 | 8 | | 55 | 13 |
| May: | 71°F | 22°C | Nov: | 60°F | 16°C |
| | 53 | 12 | | 43 | 6 |
| Jun: | 76°F | 24°C | Dec: | 52°F | 11°C |
| | 63 | 17 | | 33 | 1 |

## FLORA AND FAUNA

### Flora

In no country do flowers, plants and trees play such an important cultural role as in Japan. The Japanese innate sense of beauty manifests itself in the care with which plants are cultivated, the legends and poems which are written and such practises as **Ikebana** and **Bonsai** where the arrangement and cultivation have developed into art forms.

Thanks to the climate range there is a wonderful range of vegetation with some 5,000 to 6,000 native species of plant.

Amongst the names familiar in the West are: *Azaleas, Camellias, Flowering Cherry, Gardenias, Hydrangeas, Plums, Quinces, Rhododendrons, Willows, Wisterias and Witch Hazels* amongst the ornamental trees and shrubs; *Anemones, Chrysanthemums, Lilies, Gentians, Irises, Morning Glories, Peonies, Primroses* and *Violets,* amongst the flowers.

The trees include *Pines, Camphors, Cypresses, Japanese Maples, Larchs, Oaks and Horse Chestnuts.*

And then there is the ubiquitous **Bamboo**. In the back streets of Tokyo where there hardly seems enough room for people let alone gardens, even the poorest house will have a small clump of bamboo tucked down beside a dividing wall. Bamboo is embedded in folk lore and during the July festival of **Tanabata** (a feminine festival seeking aptitude in weaving and sewing) the bamboo leaves have wishes engraved on them and are offered up for good luck. Similarly a bamboo plant will often be planted at the northern end of a tomb seeking the same good luck but in years gone the villagers would have their name inscribed

on a leaf, blessed by a priest and wound round their bodies to cure ailments. Japanese bamboo is unusual in its lack of blossoms due to the cooler climate and when it does blossom the superstitious expect bad times to follow.

Although, sharing with many ancient cultures the worship of the forces of nature, like wind, rain and sun, the Japanese carried it even further to include the trees and flowers and the old beliefs are still evident today e.g. the practise of decorating the gates of houses with pine branches on New Year's Day to welcome the deities harks back to when the people worshipped the evergreens, such as pines, cedars, cypresses and camphors, as they believed them to be inhabited by the gods.

Other beliefs revolve around the botanical nature of plants: the **Asunaro** (of the pine family) was believed to bear flowers when a male was present and was a good indicator for a husband if he suspected his wife of cheating; the **Biwa**, the loquat, although delicious and used to brew a special wine and tea, is considered to bring bad luck (contrarily the Biwa tea is supposed to be good for you); but the rare **kuro-yuri** or 'black lily', which grows on the slopes of *Mt. Hakusan* to the north-west of Tokyo, was venerated as a re-incarnation of the maiden **Sayuri** who was slain by a jealous lover (the hime-yuri or 'lady lily' has similar importance as being formed by the tears of a sorrowing woman).

The **Chrysanthemum**, or kiku, whose perfect form was a natural for the Japanese, is the national flower, if only by default. Since the last century it has been the symbol of the

Imperial Family and is used as part of the Imperial crest. There are said to be 5000 variations of the Chrysanthemum split basically into two major types: the bush with several large flowers; and a different species consisting of hundreds of small blossoms.

The practical side of horticulture is both mental and physical. The Japanese people have an aesthetic appreciation of the simplest plant and can find beauty in a single leaf. The natural world is a recurring theme in Japanese literature and it is notable that in the **Man'Yoshu**, the country's oldest anthology of poems dating from the 8th century, 1500 of the 4500 poems in the collection deal with plants.

Artists in. using oils, water-colours and lacquer also feature the intricate patterns of flowers, shrubs and trees in their work.

The most obvious physical appreciation of nature is in the art forms of Ikebana and Bonsai.

**Ikebana** or Kado (Flower Art), the skill of flower arranging, is thought to have arrived in Japan with the advent of Buddhism in the 6th century A.D. The flowers were offered as a sacrifice and were arranged to be as pleasing as possible to **Buddha.** From this simple work came the more highly developed **Rikka** which was the specialised, artistic arranging of flowers practised for its own sake by the upper classes from the 8th to the 16th centuries. During the 15th century a Kyoto teacher, **Ikenobo Senkei**, formalised a theory of arrangement under the principle of '*Heaven, Man and Earth*', with the highest point of a vase arrangement representing Heaven, Man in the middle and Earth as the lowest point of the pattern. This was called **Kado** and a text book was published in 1470. Various schools of thought have emerged ever since. Surprisingly, flower arranging has long been popular with the Samurai and military classes.

**Bonsai** is a younger art, starting in the 13th century and reflects the Japanese love of things in miniature (like bathrooms and bus seats) and their appreciation of nature. The secret of good bonsai is to make the pint-sized trees and shrubs look strong and powerful in their own right and not just frail copies of the real thing. It is a time-consuming and painstaking job to grow and nurture the plants and trees within the confines of their small allotments. Incidentally the cleverness of the Japanese in garden design will often lead the visitor to think he is walking through a bonsai garden when, in reality, a normal garden has been created but is stocked with naturally small shrubs and plants and not those grown in the bonsai manner.

## Fauna

It is believed that Japan was originally joined to the Asian mainland via a land-bridge from Korea in the south and with another possible link over the narrow strait separating Hokkaido with Sahkalin Island in the north This theory is used to explain the similarity of Japanese animal life with that of Asia generally and the lack of any startlingly different genus of wild life although there is a vast number of endemic species.

Dangerous animals are few and far between. The last wolves in Japan were seen in 1905 and since then the only large mammals of any threat have been the *Brown Bear*, the *Himalayan Black Bear* and the *Wild Boar*.

The following groups cover the main range of wild life in Japan:

MAMMALS: There are around 110 kinds of land mammals. Apart from the previously mentioned bears the range includes *sika deer*, the Japanese serow, *raccoon dogs* (which climb trees and live on fruits although of the canid variety), giant *flying squirrels, monkeys, bristled rats, Amami spiny mice, Iriomote cats, Amami rabbits, voles, moles, shrews, bats, flying foxes, martens, dugongs, sea lions, walruses and macaques*.

BIRDS: 490 species of birds have been logged in Japan most of which are variations of breeds from China and Sth East Asia. Some of the more interesting specimens are the *Pryer's woodpecker, the copper pheasant, the Bonin honeyeater, the Japanese wagtail, the yellow bunting, Amami woodcock, the extremely rare Miyako kingfisher, the Japanese crane, the spotbill duck, an indigenous albatross, the grey-faced buzzard eagle, the bush warbler, the mandarin duck and the Japanese robin* which is called the '*horse bird*' because its chirp is like the neigh of a horse.

REPTILES AND AMPHIBIANS: 73 species of reptiles and 40 species of amphibians can be found in Japan and its waters. Although several varieties of turtles have been seen only two, *the Ridley* and *the green turtle*, actually lay eggs on Japanese beaches. The main deadly snake to be found on the main island of Honshu is *Haly's viper*. There are various other snakes scattered through the islands with the Ryukyu Islands attracting a large proportion as well as a particularly deadly skink, *the Okinawa habu*. Salamanders, newts, frogs and toads are common with the *kajikagaeru frog* being kept as a pet because of its pleasant croak.

**FISH:** the most widespread and best known of the Japanese fish is the infamous *carp* ( originally from China) which has played havoc around the world. The islands of Southern Japan with their warm tropic waters attract the most colourful coral fish as well as various sharks including the rare *frilled shark* (the Japanese prize shark fins for their edibility and will hunt in waters throughout the Pacific region for them which has alarmed conservationists already disturbed by Japan's notorious whaling methods).

As with all forms of natural life, birds, animals and fish are immortalised in the arts, traditions and legends of Japan.

At some villages and temples you may see the **Yamagara**, the fortune telling bird which has been trained to retrieve scraps of paper with fortunes written on them from a small shrine.

*Imperial Palace Tokyo*

In the **Uwajima** district of Iyo, **Shikoku**, a traditional bull fight was practised for many years. This was not the Spanish version but was one bull pitted against another and derived from the farmer's habits of matching bulls so that a pecking order could be established on the farm leaving the rest of the herd undisturbed. These bullfights were never to the death; they ended when one bull decided he'd had enough and moved off.

There are numerous stories of the influence and strange habits of *cats*. Many Japanese believed cats understood human language and in some remote villages could even talk back. In the 11th century cats were even accorded high rank at the Imperial Court and were accorded privileges not granted to other members of the court. In some rural districts whole mountains were said to be inhabited by cats who lived like humans.

Buddhist influences played a large part in shaping Japanese attitudes to animals and, like the Chinese, adopted certain animals such as cranes, tigers, snakes etc. as symbols of longevity, strength, cunning, virtue and patience. Literature and art reflect these beliefs but many a fairy story is woven around the exploits of a particular animal.

## GOVERNMENT

Japan is a state of limited constitutional monarch with sovereign power residing in the people. The Emperor is merely a figurehead and symbol of the State. Political power in modern Japan is exercised through the normal three branches of government: *the Legislature, the Executive and the Judiciary*.

Legislative control is expressed in the **Diet**, the National Parliament. The Diet consists of the House of Representatives, the House of Councillors, the Judge Impeachment Court and the Judge Indictment Committee. The major political parties with members in the House of Representatives and the House of Councillors are Liberal-Democrat, Japan Socialist, Komeito, Democratic Socialist and Japan Communist. The Liberal-Democrat and the Japan Socialist have the majority of members between them. Under the political system, the House of Representatives, whose members have a 4 year tenure, can override the actions of the upper house, the Councillors, but is also subject to dissolution by the Cabinet; this does not apply to the House of Councillors whose members serve a 6 year term.

Control over the Executive branch, which operates the administrative procedures of government, is exercised by the Cabinet and the Prime Minister who is chosen from within the Diet.

A post-war Constitution, in force from 1947, deprived the Emperor of all political power, abolished the peerage, granted votes to women, abolished conscription, pledged the country not to maintain Armed Forces (this is evaded with euphemistically named, but legal 'Self Defence Workers') and to renounce war as a means of settling international disputes, guaranteed complete academic freedom and set up a 'Bill of Rights' along Western lines.

Local government operates through 46 prefectures.

NATIONAL FLAG.
A white background with a red sun (without rays).

## Imperial Family

Until the end of World War II, the Emperor was considered a 'living god' which accorded with the **Shinto** idea of a 'king-god' as the spiritual focus of the nation. In a New Year speech in 1946, **Emperor Hirohito** (who died in 1989 and is now referred to as the Emperor Showa) renounced his divinity and with the new constitution settled into his role of symbolic ruler, not unlike the British monarchy. Nevertheless the Imperial Family has still remained a rallying point for the Japanese people although recent years have seen the emergence of a radical group opposed to any form of sovereign identity, something that would have been unthinkable in past years.

According to mythology the present **Emperor Akihito** is the 125th emperor in a line unbroken since the *Great Sun Goddess* **Amaterasu Omikiami**.

The controls exercised over the Imperial Family is best illustrated by the engagement of the Emperor's second son, **Prince Aya** in September 1989. By law the **Imperial Household Council**, headed by the Prime Minister, must agree to the marriage of any male member of the Imperial Family. In reality this is a formality but the power is still on the statute books and is still followed.

# EDUCATION

Following World War II, the Allied Occupation reformed the Japanese educational system and instituted a basic plan along American lines consisting of Primary Schools, Junior High School, Senior High School and College or University (called *Daigaku* or 'Great School' by the Japanese). In addition there is a kindergarten system as well.

The plan is dubbed the 6-3-3-4 System, a reference to the 6 years in primary school, 3 years in Junior High, 3 years in Senior High and 4 years in University.

Education for a period of 9 years is compulsory for all children from the age of six. This minimum education is free of charge for tuition and text books.

Entrance to Senior High School from the junior school is not automatic and is by competitive examination. Similar conditions apply to Universities.

Society has placed intolerable pressures on Japanese students by requiring high pass marks as a standard for jobs in the much sought-after business area. Junior students who fail to pass the senior school entrance exams have much less chance of making it into the better paid jobs. These demands and the shame which goes with failure have resulted in a stress-filled education system in which nervous breakdowns and suicides have been commonplace. The strain can be sensed in the frenetic behaviour of the young when 'letting off steam' exacerbated by the frenzied nature of television programmes and rock concerts.

The educational system is divided into public and private schools with the bulk of junior and secondary schools being public schools. On the other hand, there are nine times the number of private universities as there are public universities. Over half of the kindergartens are private.

*Tokyo University*

## JUSTICE

The Western model is also used for the judicial system.

At the top of the legal tree is the Supreme Court, an independent body headed by a Chief Justice appointed by the Emperor, and 14 other judges selected by the Cabinet.

The Supreme Court rules on constitutional matters as well as regulating the work of the lower courts.

Below the Supreme Court come the 8 regional High Courts, a myriad of District Courts, Family Courts and the general Summary Courts.

## COMMERCE AND INDUSTRY

Within the Asian region Japan has long been a major economic force. Now the country has risen to become a financial powerhouse in the world's markets.

In less than five decades from the devastation of World War II, Japan has risen to the point where she has toppled for the first time (in 1989) the powerful U.S.A. from the Number One postion in terms of national wealth based on the per capita gross domestic product.

Prior to the blitzing of World War II, Japan, in the twenty five years since the end of World War I, had built a solid base in textile manufacture, heavy industry and chemicals. The resources may have been ruined by the war but the skill and the knowledge remained. This was the base for the nation's dramatic recovery.

Within several years of *V.J. Day*, Japan had built the foundations for a formidable ship-building operation which was to make her the undisputed world leader in that area. Crude steel production consolidated her position in the heavy industry field.

Her export fortunes were enhanced with a turn-around in the car production market and the Japanese car developed an enviable reputation for quality, reliability and style. Similarly she sprang to the forefront in electronics covering computers, television sets, radios and cassette players (Sony was to add the name 'Walkman' to the dictionary). Cameras soon outstripped their sedate European rivals to the point where names like Nikon, Canon and Pentax were becoming the most used amongst top professionals.

Huge money surpluses gained from Japan's competitive export trade are being invested overseas with major holdings in land, manufacturing, banking and, particularly, tourism projects.

*Department Stores, Ginza*

The latter move shows the shrewdness of the Japanese financial mind. Realising the new found wealth had enabled more and more Japanese to travel (*especially the lucrative and expanding honeymoon market*), Japanese investors have sunk enormous amounts into hotels, golf courses, coach companies and travel agents. As a result the average Japanese tourist, having booked his tour at his local travel agent, will fly with Japan Airlines to America, Europe, Australia or Asia, be picked up at the airport in a Japanese built and owned coach, transported to a Japanese owned hotel, play golf on a Japanese ownod course and sightsee with a Japanese tour operator. The host country, delighted at the surge of inbound tourists, is often blind to the fact that most of the revenue is returning to Japan.

To what extent Japan will remain in the top position will depend on market forces and a growing backlash from countries where electorates, partly through concern at the heavy influx of foreign capital and partly through racial antagonism, are becoming increasingly vocal at the level of investment.

Agriculturally Japan is not succesful. Limited land for farming has meant most of the nation's agricultural efforts are channelled into producing basic food requirements such as rice, vegetables and livestock. Japan needs to import wheat, sugar and fruits. Wool and cotton are also major imports.

In the 'white collar' area, Japan is adept at running major finacial institutions: banking, public, private and merchant; insurance; credit lenders; and foreign representation.

## RELIGION

The population of Japan is around 120 million plus. According to statistics the number of religious adherents is 194 million. This would tend to confirm one's worst fears about statistics which, like a politician's promise, can be taken with a grain of rice. However the answer in this case is quite simple: many Japanese will quite happily follow more than one religion, for example, a great number will claim a dual **Shinto/Buddhist** belief; in addition, with some religions, the family unit as a whole is claimed for the religion of the head of the family but the individual members of the family following a different faith will also be included in their faith's numbers.

Although Buddhism has the greatest number of followers, Shinto has long been considered the official religion and Japanese generally are deemed to be Shintoists. Ostensibly there is no state religion. Following World War II, the Allied Supreme Command, banned any form of state support for Shinto together with subsidies for it and other religions. They also forbade the teaching or religion in schools. Many considered this to be an arrogant and insensitive decision. However the justification was the plan to diminish the role of the Imperial Family in the religious and social structure of a country whose political and military masters had used the peqple's idolatry of the Emperor in urging the Japanese into war and in hardening their resolve.

The action may have removed Shinto from the parliament and the education system, but the faith is still considered to be the national religion, official or not.

### Shinto

*'The way of the gods'* is an indigenous religion which developed out of a mixture of fear of the supernatural and the worship of nature which is both all encopassing and yet rather vague.

The Shintoist can worship a wide range of people and objects. They can include ancestors, gods from ancient mythology, the natural forces such as thunder, lightning, rain and sun, animals, fish and birds, trees, plants and even inanimate objects. Linked to Shinto is the Japanese ability to look beyond the mere exterior form of matter and determine a different, special entity.

There are two basic categories, Shrine Shinto and Sectarian Shinto.

**SHRINE SHINTO** was the cult-like development that came with the Meiji Restoration in the 19th century. Fostered in official and royal circles there was an intensity about Shrine Shinto which ideally suited its practise to the mind of the military.-If anything it can be likened to the British concept of 'God, King and Country'.

Unlike most other religions Shrine Shinto has no set scriptures or doctrines. Devotions are done on a casual, personal level, through communal prayer or through ceremonies and festivals designed to entertain the deities. The people are often unaware of the exact nature of their worship relying instead on that innate need mankind has to appease a Higher Force.

**SECTARIAN SHINTO** is the name given to all other forms of Shinto and reflects the tastes of the ordinary people as opposed to the ruling classes who followed Shrine Shinto. One of the offshoots of Sectarian Shinto is **Tenrikyo** which is unique for its structured doctrines. The founder was a woman, **Nakayama** who constituted Tenrikyo in 1838. The main belief is in God the Parent who designed humans to enjoy life. Unfortunately, falling by the wayside and accumulating 'mental dust', man needs to blow away that dust with prayer and good works before the final moment when all the world is saved and gather together around the **Kanrodai** , the 'terrace of nectar', which is situated at the sect's main shrine at **Tenri**.

There are a number of deities in Shinto who are referred to as **Kami**. The Kami are a mixture of natural phenomena, people and mythological gods. However, despite their importance, the Kami inspire respect rather than the solid devotion accorded gods in other religions. Chief amongst the deities is the Great Sun Goddess. As mentioned previously she is considered the ancestor, in a direct line, of the Imperial Family.

The Shinto shrine, although it may share the same grounds as a Buddhist temple, has one significant difference: it has no representation of a person but, instead, a symbolic feature such as a stone, a tablet or a sword. The actual inner shrine is generally closed and may only be entered by the priests. Guarding the entrance to the shrines are two **Komainu**, stone dogs, one with its mouth open and called **A**, the other with its mouth closed and called **Un**. These names represent the sounds of birth and death respectively. The gate, or **Torii**, also plays an important part because it is the dividing line between the everyday world and the divine world.

Upon entering the grounds of the shrine and before praying, a worshipper must first wash the hands and rinse out the mouth. You will see this done in a side building called **Chozuya**.

*Asakusa Kannon Temple*

Another striking feature of the temple grounds is a board, a pole or a tree from which are suspended hundreds of pieces of paper. On each paper is written someone's fortune which the recipient has tied here so the will be more easily seen by the Kami. At the actual entrance to the shrine is a slatted box, **Saisen-Bako**, into which the worshippers throw coins as a sign of respect, with an associated ritual of bowing and clapping the hands.

The priests of Shinto are instantly recognisable because of their robes and the distinct headgear, the *Eboshi*, which is tied under the chin.

> **INFOTIP:** Dress correctly when visiting shrines or temples. Shorts, bare mid-riffs and halter tops are frowned upon.

**BUDDHISM** has the largest number of adherents but lives comfortably side-by-side with Shinto. But it also has the structure, and the formalised doctrine the other lacks.

Buddhism, which reached Japan from India via China and Korea in the 6th century A.D., is locally divided into a number of sects. In order of 'popularity' these are *Nichiren, Jyodo, Shingon, Zen, Tendai and Nara*. For most Westerners the recognisable name here is '**Zen**'.

Four Noble Truths are the basis of Buddhist belief. These state: *Existence is Suffering; Suffering results from Craving; Nirvana is a State of Bliss following the Extinction of Cravings and Passion; and, to remove suffering one must follow the Eight Noble Ways (right views, right intention, right speech, right action, right livelihood, right effort, right mindfulness and right concentration).*

*Ginza, Tokyo*

These essential tenets are at the basis of the various Buddhist sects which differ in interpretation, practise and degrees of aestheticism. Zen Buddhists, for example, claim Zen is not a school of Buddhism but is the original of all schools of Buddhism.

Buddhist temples follow the same general plan as other such temples throughout Asia but with certain Japanese adaptations. The most obvious of these is the stupa temple building which, in Japan, has the shape of a five-storied pagoda. On a visit to one of these temples you will note the pagoda is surounted by something which looks like a radio antenna. This is a large pole encircled with nine rings and topped with a decoration in the shape of a nobleman's carriage, while the upppermost, tiny chamber represents a repository for Buddha's remains. In the associated graveyard are a number of rounded concrete figures called **Gorinto**. The five segments which make up these figures represent the five elements of the Buddhist universe: *fire, wind, water, sky* and *earth*.

**CHRISTIANITY** has a minor role in Japan. Persecution in previous centuries stopped the missionaries gaining the strong foothold their compatriots were able to establish in other Asian countries. Missionary work still operates within Japan and makes slow inroads into the entrenched Shinto and Buddhist beliefs. The dogmatic nature of Christian religions is a barrier to the Japanese who prefer a less demanding and more informal way to practise their faith.

> **INFOTIP:** Resist the temptation to pat small childrem on the head. In Shinto and Buddhist beliefs this is considered an affront to the soul.

## PEOPLE

The original aborigine people of Japan are the **Ainu** who account for only 15,000 in an overall population of more than 120 million. The Ainu, a taller, more hirsute race of Proto-Caucasian stock (possibly from Siberia), live mainly on the Northern island of Hokkaido. At one time they extended throughout the main island of Honshu.

The rest of the Japanese are collected together under the name of **Yamato**.

Many nations are believed to have contributed to the ethnic make-up of the Japanese. Early wet rice cultivation practises indicated a migration from Southeast Asia while nomadic traits reveal Mongolian ancestors. It is also believed Melanesian, Polynesian and Micronesian races helped in the early settlement of Japan.

Visitors to modern-day Japan will find many of the stereotype images are a little shaky. The perception of the Japanese as a nation of small people is being eroded with changes in dietary habits and improved living standards. No longer does the Westerner tower over the Japanese. In fact, the new generation of young Japanese are

*Shinjuku Tokyo*

surprisingly tall. Similarly, facial characteristics are quite different from the old cliche notions.

A class system does operate within Japan based on the usual grounds of birth, wealth and position. Although there may appear to be a uniformity within the work-place with management and worker united in the cause of The Company, in fact, the company ladder is a determining factor in one's social position and choice of friends. The most obvious and recurrent examples of this strictly enforced division can be seen any day when a group of businessmen meet - even the most untrained Western eye can spot the difference in attitudes within the group as determined by the bowing ceremony which so clearly 'separates the men from the boys'. The infamous ritual of the post-work drinks every evening at the local watering hole is another essential in the forced comradeship of the Japanese company structure. Wives are expected to be submissive in the old manner, learn to live with husbands who rarely see their family outside of weekends.

What is more disturbing is the segregation of the **burakumin** or 'country people' who have become the Japanese equivalent of India's 'untouchables'. In past days they were known as **Eta**, and in ancient society were the most inferior class. The burakumin were always given the meanest tasks. The tradition continues today and the leather tanning industry is considered the province of these luckless people. Rarely does inter-marriage take place and should it occur the outsider who marries a member of the burakumin will be ostracised by family and friends. Burakumin are also discriminated against in the work-force and will find it practically impossible to get employment outside their ghetto area unless they disguise their origins.

In the major cities, like Tokyo, the visitor will be surprised to see very little traditional dress. The *kimono* is seen so rarely that when one does come across a group of women in kimonos, trotting along with those quick, short steps, it comes as a novelty. The elderly will still wear it and in the **Ryogoku** area, home of the **sumo wrestlers,** the practise is common. Otherwise Western dress is the norm. With their customary neatness, the Japanese are arguably the most fashionable and stylish dressers in the world. The men generally opt for the formal, dark business suit, the women, even from the poorer classes, have a particularly natty dress sense and always look immaculate. It seems a point of honour with the young to adopt the latest trends and, when it comes to clothes, are interchangeable with youth the world over, even to the outrageous punk exhibitionists who emerge from the woodwork at weekends and holidays.

## MEETING PEOPLE

The casual foreign tourist will get few opportunities to meet the Japanese on an informal basis largely due to language problems and a natural reticence by the Japanese. If staying for any length of time it is worth joining a mixed social club.

Unless one is on very friendly terms it is rare to be entertained at home. Most guests are taken to restaurants with important business clients being taken to the best clubs which are affordable only to the rich or those on expense accounts (at some establishments a dinner can cost US$1000 a head). Those of lesser importance will often spend a night on the town doing the rounds of various beer halls. A 'pub crawl' is popular amongst groups of Japanese men when they get together so don't be surprised to find oneself suddenly propelled into an enthusiastic round of drinking 'on the run' (drinks will often be left unfinished when the group suddenly gets the urge to leave the current bar and look for fresher pastures). From 8pm onwards it is a common sight in Tokyo to see bands of merry Japanese lurching happily around the streets on what is often a nightly occurrence. Drinking is the one way the Japanese relax their inhibitions and behaviour that would be castigated normally is tolerated in those who are drunk. Don't be surprised if your hosts suddenly rise from the table and take the microphone and start singing: this is very popular and more than likely you will be required to do the same, so be prepared with a song (something other than one's National Anthem is suggested!).

**INFOTIP:** When visiting a private home do not go into the kitchen. This is considered a very private part of the house.

If one is invited home there are several important points of etiquette to remember:

*always remove one's shoes at the front door and place them pointing towards the way one has just come; never walk on the borders of the tatami mat; no hugging, kissing or touching unless on very intimate terms; do not stand too close when engaged in conversation; do not drink until all glasses are full and refill other people's glasses and not your own; wait until all the food is served before eating; dress formally; stay out of the kitchen as it is considered a private room; do not sit or stand in the alcove where the family displays its flower arrangements or art pieces; when the green tea is served after the meal it's an indication it is time to leave; a note or card of appreciation should be sent next day.*

Business men should remember to take a plentiful supply of cards. The first gesture upon being introduced is usually the exchange of cards which can take on the aspects of a poker game when a large number of people are present. The cards are swapped not just for reference purposes but also to establish one's place in the 'pecking order'. Amongst Japanese bowing is the correct form of greeting, farewell and apology, however with foreigners handshakes are now common practise.

> **INFOTIP:** Never enter a room with a tatami mat on the floor with your shoes on. Make sure they are removed before entering.

## LANGUAGE

Scholars believe Japanese to be a branch of the **Altaic** family of languages which extend from Asia across to the Baltic Peninsula. Local influences on the language include grammatical structures that bear a similarity to the Korean language and, the most obvious, the Chinese-style characters or **kanji**, the first written evidence of which date back to the 8th century A.D. Kanji is used in conjunction with two Japanese forms of characters, **Hiragana** and **Katakana**. Hiragana is a rounder, thicker character while Katakana has more austere lines.

The Romanised form of Japanese is known as **romaji.**

There are several dialects with the *Ryuku* islanders speaking a language that is noticeably different to that spoken in Tokyo.

Another interesting twist is the style adopted by Japanese women which has its own distinct characteristics and is decidedly 'feminine' when compared with the manner in which men speak (on reflection this is not that unusual - one only has to listen carefully to the use of the English language by Anglo-Saxon males and females).

> **INFOTIP:** The Japanese 'yes' often means 'no' or 'I don't know'. As the Japanese do not like to offend a visitor they will often agree verbally whilst disagreeing mentally.

Ostensibly Japanese is a hard language to learn. In reality it is easier than many would think once the student has overcome English prejudices about language, as the Japanese idiom not only has no genders but no noun, adjective or verb endings, no singulars and plurals and few irregular verbs.

Those doing any form of business with the Japanese will find a study of the language useful. Tourist need only bother with a couple of basic phrases unless undertaking trips outside the normal, organised tours; in which case it would be handy to get 'Speak a Little Japanese' (published and obtainable from Japan Airlines).

Pronunciation is relatively simple and generally foreigners can cope with the correct accent but now and then a curved ball appears and this can be embarrassing and lead to blank stares especially if one is seeking directions (e.g. the Tokyo suburb of Asakusa is not Ah-sah-koosa as one would expect but is actually Ah-sux-sa).

As a guide the vowel sounds are pronounced as follows:

| | |
|---|---|
| ah | as in char |
| ai | as in sky |
| e | as in lend |
| ei | as in play |
| oo | as in moon |
| gi | as in gift |
| u | as in blue |
| ee | as in bee |
| i | as in king |
| oh | as in flow |
| oi | as in boy |

Some useful phrases and words (phonetically - capital letters indicate stress):

| | |
|---|---|
| Good morning | oh-HAH-yoh |
| Hello | KOHN-ni-chi-wah |
| Thank you | ah-ri-gah-TOH |
| Goodbye | sah-YOH-nah-rah |
| Sorry | su-MEE mah-sehn |
| How are you? | ee-KAH-gah des-KAH |
| Yes | HAI |
| No | EE-yeh |
| Good | KEK-koh des |
| Do you understand | wah-KAH-ri MAS-KAH |
| Please assist me | teh-tsu-DAHT-teh ku-dah-sai |
| Do you speak English? | EI-goh woh hah-NAH-shi mas-KAH |
| Do you understand English? | EI-goh gah wah-KAH-ri mas-KAH |
| Call a doctor please | ee-SHAH wo YON-deh ku-dah-sai |
| English speaking doctor | EI-goh woh hah-NAH-su ee SHAH |
| I do not understand | wah-KAH-ri-mah-sen |

Numbers

| | |
|---|---|
| One | EE-chi |
| Two | NEE |
| Three | SAHN |
| Four | SHEE |
| Five | GOH |
| Six | ROH-ku |
| Seven | SHI-chi |
| Eight | HAH-chi |
| Nine | KOO |
| Ten | JOO |

*Maranouchi, Tokyo*

## LITERATURE

Considering the nearness of China and the important role she was to play in the development of Japanese script, it is quite surprising Japan's actual literary achievements did not start until a thousand years after her neighbour's. For instance, there was nothing from the same period to match the earliest Chinese poetry. Nor was there any equivalent of the Confucian Analects from the 5th and 6th centuries B.C.

The history of Japanese literature really falls into a series of periodic influences with each cycle lasting approximately 400 years.

### Yamoto and Nara Period

(c400 A.D. - 794 A.D.): This was the era of Japan's first major development in literature. **Kanji**, the Japanese script had emerged from the Chinese characters and the poets and wandering story-tellers commenced recording in permanent form the traditional tales which were their 'stock in trade'. It is interesting to note the two surviving major works from this period, the **Kojiki** (712 A.D.) and the **Nihongi** (720 A.D.), historical collections of songs and poems, were written in Chinese. Gradually a poetic style known as **waka,** based on five and seven syllabled lines, emerged and the a major selection of 4500 of these waka poems were published in 794 in a work called the **Manyoshu**.

### Heian Period

(794 - 1185): During this time Japanese literature flowered in its own right. The Chinese bias became less evident as writers moved away from the crude imagery of earlier years. In truth this was the start of a classical period with Japanese-language prose appearing for the first time accompanied by a new tradition of sophistication and aestheticism. Around 1015 at the Genji court, a lady-in-waiting named **Marasaki Shikibu** wrote the **Genji Monogatari** (lit.'History of the Genji'). This book, dealing with life at the court, has been hailed not only as a magnificent Japanese work, but also as the world's first great novel. The brilliant use of style and grammar made the book a landmark in Japanese literature (as a piece of trivia, the authoress was noted for her love of iwashi, sardines, which she would devour in great quantities, no doubt giving rise to the old myth about fish being excellent brainfood!). Other notable works from the Heian period included the poetry anthology **Kukinshu** and the so-called 'Pillow Book' which also dealt with life at court.

## Kamakura, Nambokucho and Muromachi Period

(1185 - 1603): Reflecting turbulent centuries of civil unrest and uprisings, literature took on a more serious, less lyrical approach. These years produced the **Gunki Monogatari** or 'war plays' and also saw the introduction of the famous **Noh** plays (see under 'Theatre'). Buddhism now had a firm hold in Japan with the result that Buddhist meditations and books became increasingly popular.

## Tokugawa Period

(1603 - 1868): The rise of the Tokugawa Shogunate saw a period of national unity and prosperity, an excellent climate for authors and scholars. Drama was the focus of much attention and the kabuki theatres flourished. Poetry evolved a new style called **kaiku** with its emphasis on subtlety and brevity. Chinese literature fascinated Japanese philosophers and writers, as did the ideas of Confuscius.

## Modern Period

(1868 - ): When Japan emerged from her self-imposed seclusion in 1853 it was inevitable foreign influences would shape the style of her literature. This happened in various forms ranging from writers who tried to ape the epic Russian style of Tolstoy to those influenced by the dynamism of the American school of the 1920's and 1930's. However throughout all this there still lurked in the background the traditional values, especially the almost ritualistic catharsis of self denigration. Poetry was, and still is, one of the most potent forms of Japanese expression together with the short story; these skills have been honed to a fine edge. The long, intricate novel is not the art form it is in other countries. The years following World War II initially brought a quieter, more reflective approach to literature but underneath lurked a burgeoning nationalism which found its most effective voice in the writings of **Yukio Mishima** who was to become a cult figure in both the East and the West. He solidified his appeal with the 1970 ceremonial suicide befitting the Samurai traditions he espoused. Ironically one of the most favoured forms of popular literature is the comic. A casual glance around a subway carriage will show its popularity with school children and businessmen alike. The violence of many of these comics is disturbing in an otherwise prudish nation (at least when it comes to magazines) and is starting to ring alarm bells in official quarters.

*Anemo, Cultural Museum*

## THEATRE

The modern Japanese classical theatre has evolved from the early folk and temple dances of the 8th century **Nara Period**. Although there are subordinate branches, the three main forms of theatrical expression are *Noh, Bunraku* and *Kabuki*.

**NOH**: (sometimes written as No): This is the most aesthetic and stylised of all classical drama although its origins were in the 'common' 13th century entertainments of dancing, juggling and comedy. However, during the 14th century a father-and-son combination, **Kiyotsugu Kan-ami** and **Motokiyo Ze-ami**, developed the various strands of entertainment into a series of plays which appealed to the ruling classes and were to become the favourite forms of entertainment for the great feudal warriors of old Japan. Accompanied by an orchestra of flutes and drums, the actors (all male - even the female roles) recite and chant tales of moral, spiritual or historical worth executing action through subtle gestures and the minimal use of props (a fan, for example, is manipulated skillfully to represent a dagger, a pen, a spear or even a plate). *Noh* is long on talk and short on activity giving it a special cultural significance which tends to appeal to the better educated and, therefore, it has always been considered the diversion of the upper classes.

*Ganza Festival*

BUNRAKU: The earliest puppet shows were performed by the **Kugutsu**. a minstrel-like band of Gypsies who had arrived from the Asian mainland during the Heian Period (794 - 858 A.D.). But it was not until the 18th century that the puppet entertainment, Bunraku, became something more than a popular distraction and evolved into a special art form. It differs from Western puppetry in that the manipulators appear on stage, albeit in black gowns and hoods, to work the puppets by hand and not from behind a screen using wires. The main manipulator, who will have spent decades perfecting his craft, will be assisted by two apprentices.

KABUKI: Kabuki is to the Japanese what the Music Hall was to the British and Vaudeville to the Americans....it's truly popular theatre. Within the framework of a play, or several plays, the various elements of theatre, music, drama, poetry and dance, are combined in tales that explore the social and historical life of the past. Unlike the Noh plays, Kabuki is emotional, dramatic and often far from subtle. It was always the entertainment of the ordinary people however modern trends have caught up and the number of Kabuki theatres has diminished with the new generation showing less interest in this traditional form.

The Japanese also have a taste for Western-style theatre, particularly musical comedies as many straight Western plays do not translate well. Tokyo was possibly the only city in the world where a musical version of 'Gone With The Wind' had a decent run.

## FILMS

Japanese cinema has as long a history as that of Hollywood. By the turn of the century local picture-makers were filming street scenes and short Kabuki plays. The industry was centred in two cities: Tokyo, which produced 'contemporary' movies; and Kyoto, where period costume dramas were made. The appeal of films to the intelligentsia stifled the fledgling industry as they demanded the same kind of repetitive routine they had come to expect with the legitimate theatre. However the tragic 1923 earthquake changed that when all the major studios were destroyed. To fill the gap before production could resume, foreign films were allowed into the country opening the eyes of audiences to different cinematic styles. The face of cinema changed. However one thing remained until the introduction of talkies - the *benshi*, the story-tellers who, standing in the wings, narrated the plot, with many embellishments of course, of the silent film unfolding on the screen. The benshi became more popular than the movies, commanded high salaries and even had the power to veto the showing of films they didn't like.

The first silent film was **Gosho's** 1931 production of '*The Neighbour's Wife and Mine*'. The sound era proved to be a boom time for the Japanese cinema and by 1940, 500 films a years were being made.

Post war censorship by the Allied Administration restricted the type of films that could be made; for instance, any film dealing with the old feudal ways was banned. Eventually these restrictions were lifted.

The years since have produced a number of talented film-makers most of whom are unknown outside cineaste circles. However regular filmgoers will recognise the name of **Akira Kurosawa** whose film *Rashomon* won the top prize at the 1951 Venice Film Festival, and whose output has been prolific and ingenious with such powerful movies as *Seven Samurai* (which inspired the American Magnificent Seven) and *Throne of Blood*, his awesome reworking of MacBeth. Much of Kurosawa's success was due in large part to **Toshiro Mifune**, undoubtedly Japan's finest and most important film star.

*Godzilla*, a blatantly silly horror film with dreadful animation, nevertheless became a cult movie both in Japan and in the West, inspiring a host of imitations. However not even the mighty Godzilla could stop the eventual decline of the industry as television moved in to capture the minds of the new generation. Production today is centred around more quality films with occasional 'block busters' in efforts to boost cinema audiences.

*Harazuku, Tokyo*

*Tokyo Station*

## ART

The ability to understand the Japanese appreciation of the beauty to be found in the mundane is the key to enjoying Japanese art. In the West, a leaf is a leaf and a stone is a stone. In Japan there are subtle graduations in the make-up of a leaf that can only be seen through discerning eyes; while stones have their own inherent beauty and strength which is why only the Japanese could create such a work of art as the stone garden at the **Zen Buddhist** temple in *Kyoto*

Like the Chinese art which had a major influence on the early development of Japanese paintings, to the foreign eye there is a numbing sameness about the elongated, Indian-ink portrayals of mountain peaks, pine trees, rushing waterfalls and ancient temples (this style is known as **Suiboku-ga**). But the subtle differences are there to be found. Similarly, of more recent vintage, one could audibly wonder why **Katsushika Hokusai** would bother doing 36 views of Mt. Fuji until one sees the careful arrangements and different perceptions he brought to his work (one in particular, of Mt. Fuji seen through creamy, curving waves, has become world-renowned and has been used on innumerable record covers).

A visit to the **National Museum** will expose you to the wide range of Japanese art including the traditional landscapes, the mighty murals of medieval and feudal life and the strikingly European style portraits of **Asai Chu**.

The tradition of Japanese art is rich and varied and in this category one should also include the sculpture for which they have a special talent, the fine calligraphy, the wonderful lacquer-ware and even the extremely artistic and sensitive approach they bring to flower-arranging.

## SPORT AND RECREATION

Lack of space for sports grounds, especially in Tokyo, makes it difficult for the Japanese to be as active sports participants as they would like so they transfer their enthusiasms into spirited support instead.

Baseball is Japan's No.1 sport and games are played most days of the year with the exception of winter. Night time games are particularly popular as they allow workers the opportunity to cheer on their favourite team either in person or by watching one of the many telecasts of the games. The All-Japan High School Baseball Tournament, held in Spring and Summer, is the highlight of the baseball year.

The other major sport, **Sumo Wrestling**, is unique and indigenous to Japan. The home of Sumo is the **Kokugikan,** the National Sumo Stadium at Ryogoku in Tokyo where three tournaments are held every year in January, May and September with three other tournaments held in Osaka, Nagoya and Fukuoka. To the foreign eye there is something preposterous about the great mountains of lard trying to wrestle each other but with a little patience you will find that you'll get caught up in the rituals and the skill that is involved. The senior wrestlers achieve the status of stars and it is a common sight to see fans clustered around the Stadium or walking through the Ryogoku district hoping for a glimpse of their favourite. Sumo is televised whenever matches are scheduled with one channel telecasting non-stop. This is the easiest way for the visitor to get to understand the sport.

**The Martial Arts** attract a huge number of participants with schools (dojo) ranging from just a few pupils to those catering for thousands. The five most popular Martial Arts are *Judo, Kendo* (fencing with bamboo swords), *Karate, Akido and Kyudo* (archery).

Soccer is the prime football code neither Rugby nor American Gridiron having caught on although all codes are watched on television.

The Japanese also have a passion for golf and tennis and are prepared to pay highly for the chance to play. Once again the land space problem has resulted in a limited number of tennis courts and, especially, golf courses. This means memberships are limited, bookings have to be made months in advance and, in the case of golf, the green fees and membership subscriptions are so high only the wealthy and those on company expense accounts can afford to play (in some cases it is cheaper to fly to other Asian countries or even Australia to play golf than to do so at home!).

Gambling is controlled and operated by the Government. The Japanese, who love a 'flutter', can gamble on horse-racing, speedboats, motor-bikes and bike racing as well as the national lottery. There is also a popular pinball game called *Pachinko* which is played in brightly lit and highly decorated Pachinko parlours. It is akin to the poker machine but the prizes are all small gifts such as cigarettes and biscuits - no money.

*Birds View Tokyo*

## CUISINE

Of all the world's cuisines, Japanese is the most artistic. Presentation rates as highly as the food itself and the skill in assembling the ingredients, cooking and then arranging the finished dish is on par with the complicated art of flower arranging. Even when food is served in a take-away shop the packaging is worth of Bond Street or Fifth Avenue.

Subtlety is also the keynote of Japanese cuisine and the foreign tastebud needs an 'education' in detecting the different characteristics of food that often looks the same.

Although there are scores of cooking styles the most popular categories the visitor is likely to encounter are as follows:

SASHIMI: Basically this is raw fish which may be served as an hors d'oeuvre or as a main dish. A mixture of fish, or just one fish such as tuna, is served sliced accompanied by a garnish of Japanese horse-radish and soy sauce in which is mixed a little green mustard.

TEMPURA: Introduced to Japan by Portugese missionaries in the 16th century Tempura is a meal of fish and various vegetables quickly deep fried in a light batter. The delicacy of this method of cooking will surprise those who are accustomed to the heavy-handed deep frying methods of Western cooks. The food is taken with soy sauce or in some cases just salt and lemon juice.

YAKITORI: A version of the Indonesian satay. Small pieces of chicken (other meats are sometimes used) are skewered on bamboo sticks and cooked over a charcoal fire. The flavour is enhanced by the tare or sauce which is brushed over the meat during cooking.

SHABU-SHABU: A Japanese fondue. Stock is boiled at the table in a round container with a central heating pipe fed by hot coals (very similar to the Mongolian 'Hot Pot'). Pieces of thinly sliced beef are cooked in the stock and then dipped into vinegary dips before eating.

YOSE-NABE: A stew of vegetables and meat, normally chicken, together with seafood gingko nuts and bamboo shoots. Mainly a winter dish.

SUKIYAKI: A meat dish that is extremely popular in Japan and in Japanese restaurants around then world, if only for the ceremony of preparing it at the guests' table. Sugar, mirin and soy sauce go into the stock which is boiled before adding tofu, beef and vegetables. The Japanese then dip the cooked portions in beaten raw egg immediately prior to eating, however in Western restaurants the egg is normally added to the boiling mixture.

SOBA: This gets its name from soba-ko (buckwheat flour) which is mixed with ordinary wheat flour to produce thin noodles which will form the basis of a wonderful, nourishing and inexpensive broth.

FUGU: A fish dish for those who like a touch of danger with their dining. Fugu is the flesh of the blowfish, as it is commonly known in most parts of the world. The flesh is sliced extremely thin and may be eaten raw or cooked with noodles and cabbage. There is a very real danger of death if the fish is not prepared carefully as the liver and other organs of the fish contain a deadly poison. Only chefs specially licensed by the Government can prepare Fugu. Even so, after dining on the delicacy one can sense a numbness in the lips. There are several reported deaths each year from those who have tried to prepare the dish themselves.

BENTO: The name means 'boxed meal'. The Bento meals are popular with those in a hurry. The boxes come in various sizes and can be basic wooden containers or quite expensive lacquered boxes. The meals can be ordered to suit and may contain sushi, cold tempura, pickled vegetables and small cakes. You will find Bento meals being served on longer train journeys and at take-away shops. There is a brisk trade in Bento meals for office and factory workers who have them delivered by bicycle messengers during the lunch break.

Although beer and sake are often drunk with meals when dining out, particularly at night rather than at lunch, green tea is still the most popular refreshment. A 'smoked' tea can also be served and will more readily please the palate of the visitor.

There is an etiquette to using chopsticks which should never be waved about in the air nor used to spear food. They should always be neatly placed on the chopstick rest when finished and should never be used to pull a plate across the table.

Restaurants are normally distinguished by the show-cases outside with life-like plastic replicas of the food served, together with prices. If language is a problem one need only point to the required dish. When a restaurant is open a small curtain of half-flags hangs across the entrance. Sometimes this is the only method of distinguishing an eating house from a normal residence.

Where a *tatami mat* is laid, usually in a small room separate from the main dining area, one's shoes must be removed. It is considered polite to place the shoes with the toes pointing in the direction from which one has just come.

For those who crave Western food there is a wide range of restaurants catering for Western style dishes although be prepared to pay high prices. Kentucky Fried Chicken and MacDonald's are well represented throughout Tokyo.

*Maranouchi, Tokyo*

## MYTHOLOGY

The mythology of Japan is interlinked with the growth and the beliefs of the Shinto religion. Scholars have seen the influence of neighbours China and Korea, and even Polynesia, on the myths.

Unlike many countries whose myths were recorded centuries before Christ, Japan's mythology only took a permanent form with the publication of the chronicles **Kojiki** and **Nihongi** in the early 8th century A.D.

The legends tell of the formation of Heaven and Earth out of the primeval chaos. Heaven was considered a vast region linked with Earth by a huge stairway whose base was somewhere west of Kyoto. To reach Heaven the deities would travel along a great river of stars which we in the West know as the Milky Way. The Underworld was reached through a bottomless abyss into which poured the waters of the sea and through which the sins of the faithful were also washed on the **Day of Great Purification**.

Originally there were seven invisible deities from which were born the two creators of Japan, **Izanagi**, *'He Who Invites'* and **Izanami**, *'She Who Invites'*. From their celestial loins sprang the eight principal islands of Japan known by the names of **Awaji, Oki, Tsukushi, Iki, Tsu, Sado** and **Oyamoto** (which was to become the main island of Honshu).

*Nakamise Arcade*

The prolific couple also spawned **Amaterasu** (Goddess of the Sun), **Tsuki-Yomi** (God of the Moon) and **Susa-no-wo** (God of the Underworld). It is interesting to note the Moon deity is male and the Sun deity is female unlike the mythologies of other countries where the genders are reversed.

*Amaterasu* and *Susa-no-wo* produced three daughters and five sons respectively who formed the eight land gods who became the eight ancestors of the families of the Ancient Nobility. **Ninigi**, grand-son of Amaterasu became the ancestor of the Emperors so that even today the current Emperor is considered the direct descendant of the Sun Goddess.

In addition to the heavenly deities there are vast numbers of earthly **Kami**. The Kami is less a god, more a superior being who is respected rather than given the unstinting adoration due to a god. There are over 800 Kami covering thunder, lightning, stones, rivers, grains, wind, life, hearth, highways, trees, food, rice, vegetation, echoes - in fact, name it and there is sure to be a respective Kami.

The ancient mythology is accepted, as is the way of the Shinto religion, as part of everyday life, with little real thought given by the laity to any deep religious significance. More often than not, any festivities relating to a specific god are excuses to have a good time and not occasions for soul-searching or breast-beating.

*East Gardens, Imperial Palace*

## HISTORICAL AND CULTURAL DATES

The history and culture of Japan form such a long, complex pattern that only a much larger work could possibly do justice to the subject. The following, therefore, is a surface-skimming project at best and should be taken merely as a basic primer to the events, personalities and cultural developments that contributed in some way to the physical and mental growth of Japan.

The dates have been grouped together in the major time periods of Japanese history.

At regular intervals, where appropriate, there are listed notable events from the world outside Japan, which occurred during the same period, to give a comparative framework within which to relate Japan's growth. These 'foreign' events are italicised and enclosed within brackets.

*Tokyo Tower*

## Pre-History

Accepting that early forms of man developed in the African continent it is believed that Homo Erectus moved across to Northern Asia either via the Middle East and India or up through Java. This trek took place approx. 700,000 years ago, just prior to the First Ice Age. So far the most notable early discovery of this trek was that of Peking Man unearthed at Zhoukoudian near Beijing in 1927. Peking Man, from the Middle Pleistocene era, is 450,000 to 500,000 years old.

Archaeological research indicates the presence of Man in Japan during the Paleolithic and Pleistocene periods although there has been some disagreement over the authenticity of these finds.

## Neolithic, Jomon and Yayoi Periods c.7000 B.C - 350 A.D

Although no written records are available, archaeological discoveries show the presence of Neolithic settlements. The first distinctive traces are of the **Proto-Jomon** period (or Iwajuku period from the town where early stone artifacts were uncovered). Later (c. 6000 B.C.) came the Jomon culture, which was of Caucasic origins from Northern Europe and Asia, and was believed to have moved across into Japan either via the island of Sakhalin off the north-east coast of Siberia. The present day **Ainu** race, who once occupied most of Japan but are now largely restricted to the northern island of *Hokkaido*, are considered descendants of this race. Jomon means 'cord mark' and refers to the coil-like motifs on their pottery.

660 B.C. saw the enthronement of the **Emperor Jimmu** who ruled until 585 B.C. Unsubstantiated records claim he was born in 711 B.C. thus he would have been 126 years old at the time of his death which would put him in the Moses' category. However this period is looked on as the start of the Japanese Empire.

Around 300 B.C. came the **Yayoi culture** whose artifacts show a greater degree of sophistication with clearly defined, primitive sketches of men, boats and animals. This was an agricultural civilisation and dominated Japan until approximately 350 A.D. The similarities of farming methods and artifacts strongly suggest a migration from the Korean peninsula.

Overall this was a time when early man started to consolidate his mastery of the elements. The use of tools became more sophisticated, animals were put to domestic use, the cultivation of crops increased, a primitive interest in art emerged, pagan worship took on a more cohesive

*Meiji Shrine Tokyo*

shape and interaction between tribes made mankind aware of his social condition.

The first contacts with China were made and hostilities continually erupted between Japan and the fledgling nation of Silla on the Korean Peninsula. With the arrival of an **Empress, Pimiku**, Japan became known to the Chinese as '*Queen Country*'.

**HIGHLIGHTS:** *6500 B.C. Jomon Culture.*
*660 Jimmu as Emperor, start of Japanese Empire.*
*300 Yayoi culture.*
*147 A.D. 43 years of civil war begin.*
*190 Pimiku, first woman to ascend throne.*
*255 Confucianism arrives in Japan from China.*
*(Development of pottery within the Yellow River Valley. Menes first pharoah of Egypt; earliest examples of Egyptian hieroglyphics; first step pyramid at Saqqara; megalithic tombs along Iberian peninsula and British Isles; Jericho founded; tribes spread through the Americas; invention of wheel and plough c.3500 B.C. - 2,000 B.C.; glass made in Mesopotamia, 1600; Melanesians reach Fiji, 1300; First Olympic Games, 776; Foundation of Rome, 753; Confucius born, 551; Nebuchadnezzar builds Hanging Gardens, 580; Pythagoras, 530; first books of Old Testament, 430; Julius Caesar invades Britain, 55; birth of Christ; first use of paper, 105 AD; introduction of Buddhism into China, 150; rise of Maya civilisation in Mexico, 300).*

## Early Period (350 - 710 A.D.)

The 4th century was marked by the so-called **Tumulus Period**, named for the burial mounds which had been used in western and southern Japan. This culture was akin to a similar mound-burial culture in North Korea and Mongolia. Funerary objects included jewellery and clay figures of men, women and horses (reminiscent of the famous Qing Entombed Warriors at Xian in China).

It was during this time the idea of an indigenous Imperial clan gained further strength with the establishment of the capital at Yamato. The most important cultural event was the arrival of Buddhism from China with a subsequent effect on religious practises and art. Also from the Asian mainland came Chinese script and this impetus produced the first historical chronicles, the **Kojiki** (712 A.D.) and the **Nihongi** (720 A.D.). Both were written in the Chinese script.This era was to set the scene for the important **Nara Period**.

HIGHLIGHTS: *300 Tumulus tomb culture.*
*391 Major military defeat of Silla, Korea.*
*400 Yamato Imperial Clan established.*
*552 Arrival of Buddhism.*
*594 Buddhism proclaimed state religion.*
*607 First Japanese embassy in China.*
*708 Copper found in Japan. Coins minted.*
*(Armenia is first Christian state 303; Samoans colonise Tahiti, 337; Bible translated into Gothic, 350; St. Patrick lands in Ireland, 432; death of Attila the Hun, 453; Chinese astronomers make first recorded observation of Halley's Comet, 467; maize being cultivated in North America, 490; bubonic plague in Europe, 542; death of Mohammad, 632; completion of Dome of Rock in Jerusalem, 692).*

## Nara Period (710 - 784)

Although the period covers only 74 years it was of importance if only for the ending of a long tradition of changing capitals with the accession of each new emperor as the former house was considered defiled by death. In 708 the **Empress Gemmyo** decreed that the site of the capital should be changed from Fujiwara to Nara which was completed by 710. In 784 the capital was transferred for a decade to Nagaoka before settling on the most permanent site to date, at Kyoto where it stayed until 1868. Here at Nara the capital was actually called **Heijo** or 'Peaceful Castle' a name which was belied by the series of bloody rivalries for the throne which changed hands with remarkable frequency. On a more placid note the Nara

Period did see the flourishing of Buddhism in all aspects of Japanese life and culture to the extent the wealth of the temples was eventually perceived as a threat which led to the change of capitals by the Emperor.

HIGHLIGHTS: *710 Capital moved from Fujiwara to Nara.*
*712 Publication of Kojiki,first history.*
*715 Accession of Empress Gensho.*
*720 Publication of Nihongi chronicle.*
*752 Dedication of Great Buddha at Nara.*
*765 Assassination of Emperor Jonin.*
*769 Dokyo plot to overthrow the throne.*
*(Printing develops, 730; China spreads paper making to the West, 751).*

## Heian Period (784 - 1185)

The four centuries of the Heian Period commenced with the decision by **Emperor Kwammu** to move the capital from Nara to Nagaoka. Here he created the city that was to become Kyoto and which he called Heian, *'Capital of Peace and Tranquillity'*, a misnomer if ever there was one.

As befits an era which saw increasing religious, cultural and trade ties with China, Heian was modelled on the Chinese capital of the time, Chang-an, utilising such concepts as the neat grid system of roads.

The Chinese-propagated version of Buddhism along with the Confucian ideals were to undergo changes during this time. The Japanese felt less and less comfortable with the moral and philosophical strictures of the religion. Buddhism had lost its hold on the common people and was becoming more and more an ascetic religion practised by priests and scholars. A Japanese priest, **Saicho**, developed a more palatable form of Japanese Buddhism which, in turn, was mirrored by the rise in Shinto followers who appreciated the more relaxed and easy-going nature of that religion.

The Heian Period was also a turbulent time. The growth of the powerful **Fujiwara** family and clan brought with it a luxurious lifestyle and immense influence throughout the land. Inevitably corruption and unrest were to follow and the land blazed with battles and civil wars.

Conflict over tax-free lands involved the various monasteries many of whom raised their own armies and precipitated the events which led to the fall of the Fujiwara and its replacement by the **Taira** clan.

The Taira held power from 1068 to the end of the Heian period in 1185 and in little over a century were responsible for the sudden growth of the samurai class. The samurai were a caste of military warriors who had received their name from a corruption of words meaning *'one who serves'* or *'one who is on guard'*. Entitled to wear two swords they formed the **Imperial Guard** and became the most famous symbol of Japan. It was no coincidence this century's literature was noted for its emphasis on romantic stories of great wars, chivalry and deeds of daring. Similarly, the sword took on the mystic qualities which it still enjoys today in Japan.

The Taira clan was to be replaced by the **Minamoto** which signalled the start of the *Kamakura* Period.

HIGHLIGHTS: *784 Capital moved to Nagaoka.*
*794 Heian (later Kyoto) officially created.*
*812 Final subjugation of the Ainu race in Honshu.*
*858 Fujiwara Yoshifusa becomes Regent.*
*937 Revolt of Masakado sees rise of Taira clan.*
*999 Taira rebellions in western Japan.*
*1068 Accession of Sanjo puts curb on Fujiwara clan.*
*1088 Rise of samurai class.*
*1156 Taira family domination begins.*
*1185 Defeat of Taira by Minamoto Yoritomo.*
*(Viking raids begin, 793; first book printed, 853; Charlemagne crowned Emperor of Rome, 800; Norse discover Ireland, 861; Alfred the Great revives learning in England, 891; Vikings discover America, c1000; Macbeth murders Duncan, 1040; moveable type printing invented, c1045; William the Conqueror kills Harold at Hastings, 1066; Chartres' Cathedral begun, 1154).*

*Commuters at Tokyo Station*

## Kamakura Period (1192 - 1333)

The establishment of the **Minamoto** residence in the town of Kamakura gave it quasi-capital status which was to last until the near destruction of the town in 1333.

Minamoto Yoritomo was appointed the first Shogun or '*Generalissimo*' in 1192 giving birth to the *Shogunate* form of military government in which the Emperor was basically a figurehead. The Shogunates remained until 1868.

The Kamakura Period was one of military conflict both internally and from outside. The great Mongol leader Khublai Khan, rebuffed by the Japanese when he demanded 'friendship or else', launched the first of two attacks in 1274 in which he made some inroads but was narrowly defeated. A second attempt in 1281 resulted in the destruction of his fleet by typhoons or '*Divine Winds*' which gave rise to the infamous phrase **kamikaze** from kami (divine) and kaze (winds).

Meanwhile within Japan the rise of feudalism had developed through the conflict of two ruling classes appointed by the Shogun to control aspects of the country. These included the office of Constable, or Military Governor, and *Steward*, a civil administrator. However the Stewards gradually took over various judicial roles in addition to their administrative chores and this encroached on the duties of the Constable. They both jockeyed for power, land and wealth and it is not surprising the Constables were to win in the end, becoming the major

*National Diet Building*

feudal barons of Japan while the Stewards had to be content to form a middle class of squires.

Religiously Buddhism regained its popularity amongst the ordinary people as it became less dominated by the upper and intellectual classes.

The art world saw a swing to picture scrolls. The portrait painter emerged as an important adjunct to the life of the Shogun whose ego was massaged with appropriately powerful portraits. Literature meantime reflected a new nationalism and a positive rejection of former Chinese values can be detected.

HIGHLIGHTS: *1192 Minamoto Yoritomo made Shogun.*
*1232 A more formalised code of law introduced.*
*1274 First Mongol invasion...unsuccessful.*
*1281 Mongol fleet destroyed by typhoon.*
*1333 Destruction of Kamakura during civil war.*
*(Genghis Khan captures Khanbaliq (Beijing), 1215; Marco Polo arrives in China, 1275 ; Robert Bruce king of Scotland, 1306; Black death in Europe, 1348; first Chinese settlement of Singapore 1349).*

## Muromachi Period (1333 - 1500)

This is sometimes known as the *Ashikaga Period* after the family that provided 15 shoguns who ruled from 1338 to 1573. The first of the shoguns was **Takauji** who was responsible for a series of new temples built around the country and also for the transcription of the complete Buddhist works. However he was deposed after a bitter war with his son and his brother.

Zen Buddhism gained the ascendancy during this period attracting the interest of the feudal classes who were seeking the ascetic and intellectual stimulus the military had discovered in the religion during the previous period. The monasteries attracted a number of the laity and became centres for literature and art.

At the same time a new emphasis was placed on the family as a social and economic unit and, in conjunction with this, obedience, patience, sacrifice and respect for the aged and authority became the cardinal virtues.

A ten year civil war from 1467 heralded the strife that was to follow by next century.

HIGHLIGHTS: *1338 Takauji becomes first Ashikaga shogun. 1467 Onin Civil War.*
*(University of Cracow founded, 1364; Joan of Arc active in France, 1428; Gutenberg prints first book in Europe, 1445; the Renaissance period in full flower with da Vinci, Michelangelo and Botticelli, c1500).*

*Maranoutsi, Tokyo*

## Sengoku Period (1500 - 1603)

It was called the *'Age of a Country at War'*, a reference to the civil strife that wracked Japan as the feudal barons and church leaders squabbled. The Shogun and the Emperor were powerless as the autonomy given to the regional lords enabled them to go their own way with almost total impunity. Surprisingly the major bureaucratic institutions emerged not only unscathed but strengthened by the time the smoke had cleared.

Mid-way through the 16th century Japan had her first contacts with the West following the arrival of three Portugese sailors blown off course by a typhoon in 1542. Within seven years, by the time Francis Xavier, the Jesuit missionary, had arrived, Portugese traders had reached Kyoto. Following Xavier came other Jesuit missionaries and by 1582 there were an estimated 150,000 converts. The arrival of Spanish Franciscans led to inter-religious feuds which infuriated the ruling shogun, Hideyoshi, who abrogated the tolerance with which the foreign religionists were treated and commenced a persecution which lasted until his death.

HIGHLIGHTS: *1542 First Portugese land in Japan.*
*1549 St. Francis Xavier arrives.*
*1583 Castle of Osaka built.*
*1586 Great Buddha at Kyoto built.*
*1587 Persecution of Christians by Hideyoshi.*
*1592 Hideyoshi invades Korea, reaches Pyongyang.*
*1594 Monoyama Palace built.*
*1596 Peace with Korea.*
*1598 Hideyoshi dies.*
*(The watch invented, 1509; Portugese established at Macau, 1557; defeat of Spanish Armada, 1588)*

## Tokugawa Period (1603 - 1868)

In many ways this was the most important pre-20th century period in Japan's history for out of its melting pot bubbled many of the traditions and beliefs that formulated the Japanese character we know today.

The installation of **Tokugawa Ieyasu** saw the transfer of the Shogunate to the fishing village of Edo (now Tokyo) in 1603 where Ieyasu already had his residence. The Emperor still remained in Kyoto. Not that it made any difference for during this era the power of the Emperor was reduced even further with the **Bakufu** or 'tent government' (the military) controlling every Imperial decision. This interference was to be extended to all classes of society. Rules and degrees covered every aspect of life from the clothes one could wear to the food one could eat. Religious and social contacts were controlled. Japanese society by then had evolved into four classes: nobility, military, farmers and merchants. The latter although they could control the economy with the raising or lowering of rice prices were considered the lowest group.

Persecution of Christians was renewed until all were eliminated or had gone underground. A paranoia about foreign interference, sparked by the work of the Christian missionaries, led to the Japanese government closing the country for nearly two centuries. All trade was banned, except for an initial concession to the Dutch who were allowed to operate on a limited basis through the port of Nagasaki; this was later revoked. Japanese were not allowed to travel upon the pain of death and even those who had been overseas and returned were often executed to prevent the spread of outside ideas. It comes as no surprise to learn the ritual **harakiri** sword suicide became officially recognised as a form of face-saving punishment for the samurai classes during this period.

The stifling bureaucratic nationalism was reflected in the arts with literature and painting taking on a formalised, stilted approach with no generation of new ideas.

In 1853 the American, **Commodore Perry** arrived demanding the ports be open. Yokohama and several others were re-opened but there was a three-day bombardment of the **Shimonoseki Straits** in 1864 by British, American, French and Dutch forces when the Straits were closed again.

In the meantime Imperial sentiment was growing stronger and finally the **Choshu** and **Satsuma** clans joined forces to oust the Tokugawa shogunate and permanently put an end to the power of the shoguns. The **Emperor Meiji** took over rule of the country in 1868.

HIGHLIGHTS: *1603 Establishment of Tokugawa rule at Edo.*
*1617 Further Christian persecutions.*
*1639 Seclusion edicts finalised. Country shut off.*
*1657 Great Fire of Edo.*
*1690 Excursions into Manchuria.*
*1732 Great Famine.*
*1783 Four years of rice riots over high prices.*
*1808 First attempts by British to break isolation.*
*1853 Arrival of Commodore Perry.*
*1854 Treaty of Friendship with USA.*
*1867 Abolition of Shogunate.*
*('Mayflower' lands in New England, 1620; Tasman circles Australia, 1645; execution of Charles 1, 1649; Taj Mahal built, 1653; China occupies Tibet, 1751; American Declaration of Independence, 1776; French Revolution, 1792; Great Trek by Boers, 1835; Opium War, 1839-42; Hong Kong ceded to British, 1842; Communist Manifesto stated by Marx and Engels, 1848).*

## Imperial Period (1868 - 1945)

The abolition of the Shogunate and the restoration of Imperial power was to lead Japan into the modern world. Under its forceful Emperor with his new authority, the feudal, rural-based Japan embraced the 20th century with an eagerness to modernise and expand that, ironically, was to eventually precipitate the downfall of the '**Chrysthanemum Throne**' and revert the monarchy to the status of a figurehead.

One of the Emperor Meiji's first actions was to move the Imperial Court in 1869 from Kyoto to the administration capital, Edo which he renamed Tokyo.

Meiji introduced a new constitution which changed the Throne into a constitutional monarchy with himself as Sovereign Head of State and Supreme Commander of the armed forces.

With the rapid modernisation of Japan and the change into a powerful industrial and commercial base the need for new markets, a natural bellicose tendency developed out of years of feudal conflict and right-wing nationalism amongst the army led Japan into a series of military excursions. Initially it was China and Russia, but Japan's serious intent was evident in her occupation of the old foe, Korea in 1910. For 35 years Japan's occupying forces went about the ruthless task of suppressing the Korean people and attempting to obliterate all signs of Korean culture.

The disastrous **Kanto** earthquake of 1923 was soon followed by a world economic depression. This further fuelled the strength of the army and the country's rampant nationalism then led the invasion of Manchuria in 1931 followed by China in 1937 with the violent sacking of **Nanking**. Other Asian nations followed as Japan moved into a declared war with the Allied Forces after the sneak attack on **Pearl Harbour** in 1941.

This was all done in the name of the **Emperor Hirohito** who had ascended to the Throne in 1926. Historians still debate his role in the events of World War II. Active or passive? A considerable body of opinion suggests he was the tool of the militarists who used the devotion to the Emperor, the 'Living God', to inspire the people and blind them to the consequences of the Generals' perverse ambitions.

The use of the atom bomb ended both the war and the power of the Imperial Court.

*Kodomono Shrine*

HIGHLIGHTS: *1869 Transfer of Imperial Court to Tokyo (Edo).*
*1871 Abolition of four-class feudal system.*
*1894 Sino-Japanese war. Japan victorious.*
*1904 Russo-Japanese war. Japan wins.*
*1910 Invasion and annexation of Korea.*
*1912 Death of Meiji. Accession of Taisho.*
*1914 Japan enters 1st. World War.*
*1920 Japan joins League of Nations.*
*1923 Kanto earthquake.*
*1926 Death of Taisho. Accession of Hirohito.*
*1931 Japan invades Manchuria.*
*1933 Japan withdraws from League of Nations.*
*1936 Military nominate new cabinet.*
*1937 Invasion of China.*
*1940 Alliance with Germany and Italy.*
*1941 Attack on Pearl Harbour.*
*1945 Atomic bombs on Nagasaki & Hiroshima.*
*(Commonwealth of Australia declared, 1901; Wright Brothers' flight, 1903; World War 1, 1914-18; League of Nations established, 1920; Wall St. crash , 1929; Hitler made Chancellor of Germany, 1933; Spanish Civil War begins, 1936; World War 11 1939-45).*

## Post-War Period (1946 - )

The immediate post-war years were devoted to reconstruction: physical, mental and social.

One of the first tasks of the Occupation Administration was to divest the Emperor of this god-like image. Hirohito himself announced he was not the 'Living God'. Similarly Shintoism, the former State Religion and faith of the nationalistic military, was relieved of its official status. The new constitution forbade armed forces as such, although a defence militia serves the role.

Within seven years the Americans ended their occupation although they still maintain a presence. With the withdrawal, the Japanese single-mindedly set about re-establishing themselves as a financial and trading power. In less then forty years Japan has become the most important economic force in the world. The one-time imitators have become the innovators.

This achievement has not been without its problems. The pressure to succeed is causing enormous tensions within the young and there are signs of a growing backlash against the hidebound traditions of unquestioning loyalty and obedience. The scramble for dollars has left a trail of private, public and political corruption. There is even a whiff of a resurgence of nationalism as activists promote a return to the older, simpler life in the face of Japan's rampant materialism.

The death, in 1989, of *Emperor Hirohito* severed the umbilical cord with Japan's unusual recent history of power, pride, devastation and humiliation. Japan's future course towards the Year 2000 is now more important than ever, not just to the Asian region, but to the whole Western world.

HIGHLIGHTS: *1945 American Occupation.*
*1947 New constitution. Women get the vote.*
*1952 End of American Occupation.*
*1956 Japan joins United Nations.*
*1972 Okinawa restored to Japan.*
*1972 Japan renews relations with China.*
*1989 Death of Hirohito.*
*1989 Japan tops world's economic ladder.*
*(Declaration of People's Republic of China, 1949; death of Stalin, 1953; Sino-Soviet split, 1960; building of Berlin Wall, 1961; Yuri Gagarin, first man in space, 1961; John F. Kennedy assassinated, 1963; China's Cultural Revolution, 1966; U.S. withdraws from Vietnam, 1973; Watergate, 1974; death of Mao, 1976).*

*Harijuku, Dept. Store*

# PART II
## Sightseeing

Tokyo Tower & Shiba Zoojoji Temple

# TOKYO

## INTRODUCTION

Visitors to Tokyo tend to let the sheer size of this city, the huge population, the language and the 'foreignness' obscure the fact Tokyo is easy to explore on one's own.

It's too convenient just to book one of the daily coach tours and let a manufactured Japanese 'experience' cocoon one in that comfortable, warm blanket where there is no need to think, just look. But, like getting up in the morning, it doesn't take much of an effort to throw off that blanket and to lurch out into the real world. After the initial 'shock' you will find it's quite pleasant out there.

But while one can't ignore the dimensions of Tokyo it is simply a matter of learning to live with its size and making its advantages, e.g. make the excellent urban rail system, work for you, and not the other way round.

Sightseeing in Tokyo requires preparation. There is no point in launching out into the hurly burly of the city and hoping for the best. Confusion, anxiety and disappointment will be the only results. This means investing a little time in organising a plan of 'attack'. The following steps should help ease the burden:

1) The most sensible approach one can take to exploring Tokyo is to decide to tackle the city in small sections rather than as a whole.

2) Select the sights and the areas which take your fancy. Divide a map of the city roughly into the four quarters of the compass and apportion the sights accordingly. Try for a balance in your sightseeing. One can rapidly get 'temple fatigue' after the tenth visit to a religious shrine. If you hate museums don't feel you have to see them just to impress your friends (there are some unusual 'special interest' museums in Tokyo which are worth seeing even by the most die-hard museum loather). Remember, you are paying for the trip so please yourself and not others.

3) Prepare a detailed transport plan. For a start forget about hiring a car. From a foreign driver's point of view the sameness of the streets, the vague English road signs and the volume of traffic make driving an exercise in futility. The train system is the only way to go. However, you will need to study a map of the rail network to decide which of the 14 different lines you will need to use. In a notebook plot your itinerary station by station and line by line (the rail

maps colour-code the various lines which are all privately owned). Rarely will you be able to use the one line to reach all destinations so be extremely careful. Take the notebook with you on your daily forays - it will make the daunting business of rail travel a relative breeze.

4) Along with the notebook pack a few calming thoughts. There are so many people thronging the streets, the shops and the stations there is an alarming tendency to experience claustrophobic panic. When you start to feel that it is all getting too much, take an instant 'breather': stop for a moment, take a few deep, slow breaths and mentally unwind. If necessary find a cafe and relax over a 'cuppa'.

5) Don't do too much. A walking tour is tiring. Make sure you have finished by mid-afternoon before the peak hour train rush (although every hour may seem like peak time in Tokyo, there are definite morning and evening hours when mere bedlam becomes chaos!)

6) If you think you will need a taxi to return to the hotel ensure you have sufficient cash and get the hotel concierge to write the hotel's name in Japanese on a card - few of the taxi drivers speak English.

7) Be willing to deviate from the straight and narrow. Surprises await around every corner in Tokyo so be prepared to wander down little streets that look interesting but take careful note of any landmarks so you can easily return to the main route.

8) On the spot help can be provided by the **Japan National Tourist Organisation** through a series of 'Tourist Telephones' located in major areas of Tokyo.

These are just some basic rules. You will soon adapt them to suit your own needs. The important point to remember is, Tokyo is a city to be enjoyed; it is not a fearsome monster waiting to devour unsuspecting tourists.

Nevertheless it is necessary to remember Tokyo is basically a new city, despite its age. The destruction of the last war left Tokyo only the bare bones from which to re-construct. Don't expect to find history lurking around every corner. Certainly there are a number of the old, traditional homes tucked away in the urban sprawl of the city but you won't be swamped with that sense of the past that you would find, for example, in Kyoto. The most notable exception is the Imperial Palace which survived the

American bombing due, it is believed, to instructions issued lest the killing of the Imperial Family provoked intolerable resistance.

Notwithstanding, what Tokyo loses on the swings she picks up on the merry-go-round. One thing which will impress the first-time visitor particularly, is the sense of serenity to be found in the midst of this hectic city. It is not only in the parks and small lakes that one can find amidst the clutter of high-rise, office buildings. It can also be found in a small alleyway where a local resident has planted a stand of bamboo that flutters gently in the afternoon breeze. A hundred metres away the main avenue will be an uproar of traffic, but, such is the atmosphere the Japanese can create in the unlikeliest locale, one could be in a rural village.

This ability of the Japanese to look for, and find, tranquillity in the midst of turmoil is one of the joys of Tokyo.

> **INFOTIP:** Finding one's way around Tokyo from an address is practically impossible. Any address given generally refers to a district and not a street. The easiest way is to ring beforehand and get directions.

*Ginza Tokyo*

To guide you around this large and fascinating city the plan is to steer you in an anti-clockwise direction using the central Tokyo station as the pivotal point and then following a route that will cover the Southern, Eastern, Northern and Western regions, in that order. If you look at a map and trace a line that joins the *Imperial Palace, Ginza, Tsukiji, Akihabara, Asakusa, Ueno, Waseda, Shinjuku, Harajuku, Shinagawa and Shimbashi* you will have the general idea of this section of the book. Naturally there will be deviations along the way as we explore the major sights worth seeing in Tokyo.

## CENTRAL TOKYO

For the purposes of this book let's define Central Tokyo as the area within the immediate vicinity of the main **Tokyo Station**.

Although it could be called the hub of Tokyo, the Tokyo Station is far from being the busiest. It handles a mere million passengers a day compared to the 8 million who bombard **Shinjuku**. Neither is it the most handsome of stations but there is a charm in its quaint ugliness that is lacking in the other above-ground stations in the city.

The building was designed by architect **Kingo Tatsuma** using the Amsterdam station for his inspiration. It went into use in 1914. For such a highly visible building Tokyo Station has weathered the war and the catastrophic 1923 earthquake. Renovations were made to the facade after World War II with one of the additions being an unimpressive, modern iron awning, completely out of character with the solemn red brick edifice onto which it was tacked.

Although not visible from outside, there are two domed rotundas over the south and north entrances (originally the south was used for entering the station while the north was for exiting; nowadays they serve both purposes).

The Japanese have a delightful propensity for defying conventional ideas and looking outside the normal utilitarian uses of public buildings like stations. Tokyo Station is a very good example of how to transform the mundane. With the 1987 privatisation of Japan National Railways the station master was given wider scope to improve the drab interiors. Since then an art gallery has been established on an upper floor in which during the winter months classical concerts are performed at the north entrance.

Of much older vintage, however, is the **STATION HOTEL**, which is distinguished by the elegant, entrance canopy on the western side of the station (it is actually part of the station building). The hotel opened at the same time as the station and its staff were used to train Japan Airlines cabin crew in the niceties of service when the airline first started. It is one of a handful of hotels in the world to be in a station proper. Rates are reasonable by Tokyo standards and the location is ideal - at least one should never be late for a train!

Tokyo Station borders the **Maranouchi,** a cosmopolitan district of broad avenues and small tree-lined streets weaving through rows of solid office buildings but without those awesome canyons of steel and concrete that dwarf one in cities like New York. As there is little shopping here the streets are less crowded so the Maranouchi can seem quite aloof from the normal hustle of Tokyo. Maranouchi is the financial hub of Japan. Those sturdy buildings house the head offices of banks, insurance companies, investment offices and several major corporations. This would be the 'Grey Flannel Suit' heart of Tokyo except it is de rigeur for the Japanese executive and office worker to wear black or dark blue, but the manufacturer who turns out white shirts must make a fortune.

*Sakura Damon Gate*

Last century, the land on which the corporate fiefdoms of Maranouchi now stand belonged to the military and was known as 'Gambler's Field' being the haunt of the less salubrious characters of old Tokyo. When the land was offered for sale in 1889 the Imperial Family were given the first option to buy. However, lack of funds prevented the Emperor from taking up the option and instead the land was sold to the Mitsubishi Company which had already established itself as a major market force. By 1894 the first building had been erected as part of a commercial development modelled along the lines of London's Lombard Street. None of those buildings remain.

Take any of the streets heading west from Tokyo Station through the Maranouchi and within three or four blocks you will reach **Hibiya-dori Avenue** on the western side of which is **Hibiya Park** and further beyond are the vast walls which indicate the Imperial Palace.

**INFOTIP:** Don't be alarmed to hear bird calls or music when you use pedestrian traffic lights. These sounds are there as an aid to help you cross the road.

## Hibiya Park

Designed and built in 1903 as the first Western style park in Japan. As well as the expanses of neatly kept lawns, flower-beds and fountains there is also a library together with a hall for cultural performances and the *Matsumotoro Restaurant* which apparently was famous for its curries with a special attraction being an annual charity day in which the curries are practically given away. The better rooms in the famed *Imperial Hotel* look out over Hibiya Park the sight of which should do much to sooth the nerves after getting the bill. Long considered Tokyo's top hotel, the current Imperial is actually the third building to serve as a hotel on that site. At the end of the last century the first Imperial Hotel was built only to be destroyed later by fire. The second hotel was the work of the noted architect *Frank Lloyd Wright* but this was then demolished in 1968 so a more modern hotel, with better facilities, could be erected. A new tower has since been added but the rooms there have an air of pre-fabricated impermanence and are rather small, so do opt for the main building if you select the Imperial Hotel (and if your bank manager agrees!). Nevertheless the service is splendid even down to the immaculate young ladies whose sole duty is to stand at the elevators, press the button for you and then bow you in or out of the lift. The hotel also has the advantage of being within a few minutes walking distance of the fashionable shops of the **Ginza**.

*Hibiya Park*

## Imperial Palace

The true centre of Tokyo. In the old days it was used as the dividing line between the **Yamanote** area, which was the more fashionable 'uptown', and the **Shitamachi** district which was the 'downtown' region between the Palace and the Sumida River.

Before being commandeered by the **Emperor Meiji** for his official residence and called the Tokyo Castle, the Palace was known as **Edo Castle** (Edo was the original name of Tokyo) and was controlled by the Tokugawa shogunate. The first castle was built by the **Tokugawa Ieyasu** when he selected Edo for his residence in 1590. For 260 years it was to be the seat of the shogunate. Repeatedly it was destroyed by fire or war and rebuilt.

The Palace, or Castle, was always impressive. As constructed by Tokugawa Ieyasa, Edo Castle was considered the largest in the world and boasted some 99 gates, which, when you think of it, was not a good idea considering the defensive nature of the castle. Regrettably, of the gates that remain today, most are closed to the public and it is not possible to see the Palace buildings unless you happen to be part of the crowds who are allowed in on the two annual occasions (January 2nd. and the Emperor's Birthday) when the ordinary people are allowed to congregate under the Emperor's balcony to offer their greetings. It is interesting to note, high office blocks which can look down on the private quarters of the Imperial Palace are not allowed to have windows in that section of the building. However the **East Imperial Garden** is open daily, admission free, with entrance through the **Otemon**, which was the former main entrance to the Palace. Of particular interest are the 19th century guard houses near the entrances with their tiled, curved roofs and dark-timbered walls. The gardens themselves are pleasant but are not essentially different from any 'non-royal' park. A few remnants of the old armories and watch-towers can be seen.

Outside the Imperial East Garden you can hire bicycles for rides around the Imperial Palace Complex which is roughly 5 kilometres in circumference, or, if you feel less energetic, you can ride along the front of the gardens to Hibiya Park passing the official entrance to the Palace and the **Nijubashi Bridge**, or Double Bridge which referred to an older bridge which had two levels both of which have been destroyed.The name is still appropriate as there is both a steel and a stone bridge at the spot. Slightly to the south of this bridge, at the southern end of the Imperial Palace Plaza, is the impressive **Sakuradamon Gate** with its stone walls, standing 'four square and solid' arising from the waters of the moat that encircles the Palace. this would be the most photographed section.

## Ginza

The Western media often refers to the Ginza as though it were one street when, in fact, it is a whole district, although quite small, in an area to the south-east of the Imperial Palace on the other side of the railway line.

The name 'Ginza' roughly translated means 'silver workers' and was an office held under the Tokugawa Shogunate to look after the coining of silver. The silver mints in the region were moved at the start of the 19th century and the Ginza reverted to a basic residential district. A fire in 1872 which destroyed most of the housing followed by the establishment of the country's first rail line which ran to Yokohama from Shimbashi on the outskirts of the Ginza was the impetus needed to turn the area into a mercantile centre. Gas lights Tokyo's first pavements as such were built alongside streets that had been constructed along the grid system. Horse drawn trams appeared.

In their enthusiasm for things Western, the Japanese developers modelled the main street, the **Chuo-dori**, after London's Regent Street. And if you can ignore the Japanese signs and faces you could very well agree they have succeeded except the Chuo-dori is far cleaner, neater and more prosperous than Regent Street. As with most things the Japanese imitated down through the years they managed to improve on the original.

Along the Chuo-dori one can spend a few hundred yen on a McDonald's 'Big Mac' or a few hundred thousand on *Mr Mikimoto's* famous pearls. The avenue is dominated by the major department stores like *Matsuzakaya* (the first in the country to allow customers to keep their shoes on - which must have been a boon in summer!), *Mistukoshi* and *Wako* whose clock tower, built in 1932, has become a recognisable landmark and is the popular meeting spot. All the department stores have large food halls located in the basement and tourists have quickly cottoned on to the fact that the many tastings available in the food departments can provide a free meal when one is counting the yen. The world famous (and expensive) cosmetic company *Shiseido* started in the Ginza in a small pharmacy opened in 1872 by **Fukuhara Akinobu**.

A good time to visit is on Sunday afternoon when the whole length of Chuo-dori Avenue is closed to vehicles and becomes one giant mall. Street stalls are set up and the crowds throng in from the suburbs making for some of the liveliest entertainment you will find in Tokyo.

In the several blocks between the Churo-dori and the Yurakucho Station are concentrated the greatest number of art galleries in the world, per square kilometre, with over 300 crammed into the area. Many of these do not function in the Western style but are, in fact, rented by artists to display and sell their own work or that of their friends. There are also the more traditional galleries which offer a range of art from the traditional Japanese to modern European together with some rather eclectic sculptures. On a more materialistic note is the Sony Building with its own 'art' displays of the latest in electronic marvels. At the nearby *Marion Building* is a glockenspiel style clock whose face raises on the hour to reveal a small set of figures which emerge to play tiny instruments.

As you move further south from the Ginza you enter the true Shitamachi district.

*Shitamachi*, or 'down-town', was used originally in the 17th. century to designate the land below the Castle Edo nearest the **Sumida River** and the Bay. It was swampy marshland and was left for the ordinary people to inhabit while the aristocracy, the samurai, occupied the higher land beyond the Castle in the opposite direction.

In some ways little has changed in 300 years, at least in concept. The district is still the province of the workers rather than the bosses, although the area provides a good living for the businessmen who control the companies and factories here.

The Shitamachi domain basically extends along the Sumida River and inland towards the west from the river, covering the precincts of *Tsukiji, Nihonbashi, Akihabara, Ryogoku, Asakusa, and Ueno*.

## Tsukiji

Tsukiji could well be the gumboot capital of the world for not only are they sold here in great quantities but are also worn by the hundreds of workers at the Fish Market. But, before we get to the Fish Market, there are one or two other sights along the way.

Tsukiji is within a few minutes rides of the Ginza on the Hibiya Line subway (the second station after the Ginza). The district is on reclaimed land (Tsukiji means 'reclaimed land'). Following the disastrous fire of 1657 which destroyed two-thirds of Tokyo, the *Tokugawa Ieyasu* turned disaster into an advantage by taking the opportunity to build a new and greatly expanded city by draining and filling the marshlands and creating a new region for residential and trading purposes.

Although Tsukiji is held up as the epitome of the *Shitamachi* lifestyle, in the early reclamation days the reverse was true. The Shogunate had handed out parcels of land to the nobility and for the use of temples. Many a mansion was built here for a daimyo (feudal lord) and thus it seemed only natural that Tsukiji should become the site of the first Foreign Settlement when the country emerged from the tortoise-shell of its self-imposed isolation during the middle of the last century. Diplomats and foreign missionaries settled on land which is now the site of the Wholesale Market. In a well meaning, but misguided attempt to please the foreigners the government, in 1869, opened the **Shibaura** pleasure centre which was several blocks populated with geisha houses. This being Victorian times, in more ways than one, the gesture was not appreciated and the ladies eventually took their charms elsewhere.

Here also, in a mansion owned by **Lord Okudaira**, were

given lessons in Western sciences and the Dutch language by **Fukuzawa Yukichi**. These private lessons in 1858 were to lead to the founding of the **Keio University** which is now situated at Mita. A memorial stone, at an intersection just by St.Luke's International Hospital, carries the words of *Fukuzawa:' Heaven created no man above another, nor below'*.

The fisherman of the district who had built their homes on the banks of the **Sumida River** also left their impression. When leaving the Tsukiji Station turn to the left and explore some of the back streets on the opposite side of *Shinobashi-dori Avenue* which will eventually lead to the Sumida River and the **Tsukudajima Bridge**. Cross over the bridge and you will find yourself in a fascinating area of fishermen's homes and shops many of which have changed little since the old Edo days. This part of Tsukiji was in fact a self-contained island until recent reclamation joined it to the mainland. Tsukudajima is famous for a dish called **tsukudani** which is a concentrated stock of fish or seaweed which has been boiled down over a period of hours in soy sauce. The concentrate is then used on boiled rice or spread on buttered toast. The smell pervades the air along with the normal aromas of fish and sea.

In the middle of July, the residents of Tsukudajima present the **Bon Dance**, an ancient, semi-religious ceremony during which it is believed the souls of one's ancestors come back to join in the songs and dances. The ceremony is called the Bon Dance and has been listed as an **Intangible Cultural Asset** by the local Tokyo administration. It takes place from July 13th to 15th in the evenings.

Now if you return to Shinobashi-dori Avenue to the pedestrian overpass opposite the station you will see the **Tsukiji Honganji Temple**. The immediate reaction is to think it is an Indian Hindu rather than a Japanese Buddhist temple because of the Indian-style architecture. This was due to the work and travels of its designer **Dr Ito Chuta** who has tried to stress the Indian beginnings of Buddhism. The temple, built in 1935, is on the site of previous temples going back to the 17th. century. You enter across a large, paved compound and the two most noticeable features, once inside, are the air conditioning and the massive gold gates that screen the innermost altar.

**INFOTIP:** Lack of English signs at railway stations make it hard to determine the exact fare. Take a guess as you will be able to pay any extra at a Fare Adjustment Office at the other end. However if you pay too much you won't get a refund.

From the temple keep walking south along Shinobashi-Dori and with a block you will reach the start of the **Tokyo Central Wholesale Market**. Tiny stalls line the street fronting the market which extends behind the shops in a labyrinth of alleyways overflowing with produce vendors. Here the local housewife can buy all the basic necessities for the kitchen: fruits, vegetables, spices, kitchen utensils, plates, chopsticks, seaweed and, of course, fish, fresh and dried, from slimy looking squid to filleted slices which will end up in that night's sashimi. Also lined up in neat rows are hundreds of gumboots which the workers at the **Fish Market**, by necessity, have to wear. The daily fish auction attracts regular sightseers, which is not particularly amusing for the buyers who throng the vast warehouse inspecting the boxes of fish which have arrived during the night from all over Japan. Around 5 am the auction begins and the Japanese version of Hell erupts as the buyers shout and shove trying to catch the eye of the auctioneer as they make their bids using their fingers in frantic movements. If you do make the visit remember these men are trying to make their living so don't get in the way apart from anything else there is the danger of getting run down by fast moving trolleys and the chance of being '*sashimi-ied*' by the knives of the workers cutting up the huge tuna. An hour after the fish auction their is the fruit and vegetable

*Ikebukuro, Tokyo*

auction which is only slightly less restrained. But even if you don't feel like rising that early in the morning (many of the trains are not running before 5 am anyway) a walk through the market later in the day is still fascinating and a little less dangerous.

After leaving the markets keep heading in a southerly direction. The walk is past an uninteresting group of market buildings and warehouses although, on the right, you will see the offices of the Asahi newspaper group.

The road curves around and shortly afterwards, on the left, comes to a small bridge over the Sumida River which leads to the entrance of the **Hama Rikyu Gardens**. These gardens were once part of the home of a Tokugawa noble family and a walk through them will justify the pride they took in the gardens. Today, especially, with the noisy fish market just across the river on one side, while large office blocks border the other side, the spread of lawns, trees and gentle slopes around the tidal pool in the centre provides a delightful spot to rest and absorb a little calmness with just a dull mutter in the background to remind us that we are still in a part of a busy metropolis. There is a statue or two but as all signs are in Japanese it is hard to fathom which is which.

In the gardens is a landing jetty for the ferries which ply the Sumida River and this makes for a natural and pleasant continuation from the walk through Tsukiji.

*Nakamise Street, Tokyo*

## Sumida River Cruise

Unfortunately many of the group tours don't feature this trip preferring to concentrate on less time consuming excursions and yet the 45 minute journey provides a different way of seeing Tokyo and can easily be combined with the walking tour of Tsukiji described above.

With the Sumida River it is a case of a '*rose by any other name*' for in its time the river has been called *the Nakatsukawa, the Arakawa, the Okawa, Asakusagawa* and the *Miyatogawa.*

Between *Takeshiba Pier*, where the Sumida joins Tokyo Bay, and the *Asakusa Pier*, upstream, there are ten different bridges one of which, the Kyosu Bridge was based on a drawbridge which crosses the Rhine River in Germany. Going upstream the bridges are: **Kachidoki, Tsukuda-Ohashi, Eitai, Kiyosu, Shin-Ohashi, Ryogoku, Kuramae, Umaya, Komagara** and **Azuma**. Further along there are another 17 bridges.

*Sumida River, Tokyo*

The real interest is the chance to look into Tokyo's 'backyard' although the old waterfront homes have largely disappeared along this stretch of the river but you will glimpse them up the side canals which help give this part of Tokyo a mini-Venice feel. Much of the waterfront is now lined with ultra-modern condominiums and apartments which give their occupants a feeling of space, something certainly lacking in this city.

As a side comment, the ferries carry the laudable slogan '*May Peace Prevail on Earth*' although this tends to be ignored by the lunchtime travellers with their food boxes who cheerfully toss their used chopstick out of the forward windows only to have them blow back in through the rear windows spearing hapless tourists.

An annual summer treat is the **Sumidagawa Fireworks Festival**.

At Asakusa as you alight take note of the large, black-glassed building on the opposite side of the river. It is topped with a giant carrot, painted gold. This apparently is one of the new breed of beer halls which have become immensely popular with the up-and-coming executive who has yet to get the key to the executive washroom along with the expense account that will enable him to fraternise at the horrendously expensive clubs and bars of the Ginza and Maranouchi districts. There seems to be no rational explanation why a carrot was chosen to advertise a beer hall.

## Asakusa

Asakusa is an excellent example of the Japanese ability to accept the co-existence of religion and Mammon in close proximity. There is none of the 'money-changers-in-the-temple' abhorrence which is the normal reaction of Western religions when trade invades the precincts of the church.

In the days of the Edo period, Asakusa was a small village near the Sumida River; the only claim to fame having been the discovery in the river of a statue of Kannon, one of several forms of Buddha. This statue formed the basis for the Sensoji Temple or, as it is popularly known, the **Asakusa Kannon**. The small gilded statue is supposed to be in the temple and although no worshipper has ever seen its existence is never questioned.

With the *Tokugawa Ieyasu* in power the sleepy hamlet was to change into an important and thriving part of the Edo capital. In a move to keep the merchants' minds on their work, the shogunate moved the entertainment district from the capital to Asakusa and further out to Yoshiwara which became the licensed brothel district.

Asakusa, thus developed, not only as an important centre of worship but as an out-of-town fun spot where the tired businessman of the day could kick off his geta (sandals) and let his hair-piece down. It was only a matter of time before the merchants decided to set up business ventures at Asakusa setting the scene for the town's eventual emergence as a major commercial adjunct to Edo and then as the modern, glittering, mini-city it is today.

Visitors are less interested in this side of Asakusa as they mainly come here to see the temple but inevitably will be caught up in the commercial side.

The Asakusa Kannon temple is the most popular in Japan. Tourists from round the world, even if they have never heard of it, will inevitably find their way here as the temple is on every scheduled city sightseeing tour....it's almost compulsory. Larger numbers of Japanese, from Tokyo and the rural districts, will make a pilgrimage too, but not for the same reasons. Despite its tourism appeal, it must be remembered, the temple is a 'working' shrine which is visited mainly for worship.

To reach the entrance upon leaving the Sumida River ferry terminal at Azuma Bridge or the nearby Asakusa Station (Ginza subway line), simply walk straight ahead over the busy six-way intersection and down Asakusa Street where, slightly recessed from the road, is the *Kaminarimon Gate*. It's hard to get lost...just follow the crowds. Now once through the gate, a tall archway common to all temples and guarded by statues of the gods **Fujin** (Wind) and **Raijin** (Thunder), you will then have to run the gauntlet of the **Nakamise Shopping Street**. This is a long walkway covered over with gold awning. Bright lit, Nakamise extends for several blocks and every square metre is occupied with a shop or stall. It is amazing what you can buy here. As well as incense sticks for the worshippers, there are souvenir shops, fashion and jewellery boutiques, shops crammed with toys, restaurants, chopstick sellers ....you can even buy wedding dresses.

At the end of Nakamise Street is another large archway, the **Hozomon Gate**. To the left is the **Five Story Pagoda** which was rebuilt in 1973. The Pagoda is topped with a metal tower which looks like a small radio or television mast. This is part of the essential decoration and consists of a central pole encompassed by nine rings known as Horin. At the base is a Ukebana, a flower shaped decoration,at the top has a Suien, representing a nobleman's carriage. The peak is crowned with a Hoju, a tiny chamber for Buddha's remains. On the other side of the square, directly across from the Five Story Pagoda is a small cemetery and shrine.

In the courtyard before the main temple you will notice a large incense burner around which there are continual groups of Japanese who appear to be fanning themselves. Actually they are waving the smoke from the incense across their bodies. The smoke from the incense is believed to be imbued with sacred powers which will help heal the sick and make the weak strong. Also nearby is the water containers where the devout drink from ladles in a ritual purifying of the mouth.

Here, as in other temples, you will see the walls and the pillars 'decorated' with pieces of paper which have been stuck on. This is the practise of **senjafuda** which consists of the name and address printed in a special calligraphy and left at the temple as proof of one's visit. The practise dates back centuries but has become such a nuisance, like graffiti, it has been banned in most places. However so popular is senjafuda, that parties are held to ritually exchange names (in the business world the flurry of business cards produced at one's first meeting is the modern equivalent).

The **Hondo** or Main Hall of the temple is not the original building which was destroyed by fire during World War II. The present structure was completed in 1958. It is vast in size and is always thronged with worshippers. In the innermost recesses is the Kannon, the golden statue, which is never put on display. A legend attached to the Kannon tells of a golden dragon which came down from heaven at the time the statue was first enshrined at the temple. This belief is commemorated with an annual dragon dance.

Upon leaving the temple avoid the crowded Nakamise Street and leave by one of the side exits. As this is the main entertainment area of Asakusa you have a choice of the modern or the traditional. Within a block of the northwest corner of the temple grounds is the **Hanayashiki Amusement Park**, mainly for children, with several fun fair rides, but there is also quite a pleasant garden for the parents.

In the days of the Edo Period, the Hamayashiki site was a popular place for outdoor entertainment. Wandering puppeteers would act out legends and mythical stories and performing monkeys were also popular. The fair ground was destroyed during the last war but was re-constructed shortly afterwards. Entrance is free but the rides and attractions all charge a fee. As well as the normal amusement park rides there is also a Panorama Hall displaying photos and exhibits of Asakusa's past.

Alternatively the parents may find themselves at *Ichimon* on the Kototo-dori Avenue which runs along the north edge of the Park. Ichimon is a bar and restaurant popular with the locals and has a unique system of in-house currency which consists of small wooden markers known as mons which you purchase upon entering and then use for food and drink.

South of the entertainment park are several blocks which make up the Rokku district, famous in the old days for its theatres and, more recently, movie houses. Sushiya-dori is the main thoroughfare of the Rokku and has blended in with the rest of Asakusa with its department stores, shops and garish posters. However if you wander off the Sushiya-dori down some of the narrow laneways it is still possible to come across the occasional example of the old homes of the Meiji period. Unfortunately they are few and far between as both war and progress have seen their replacement with shops or more modern dwellings. Japan's first permanent movie theatre was established in the Rokku district in 1903 and during the days of the silent films the Japanese were able to adapt their love of story-telling to the new medium by hiring narrators to stand in the wings and tell the plot of the film unfolding on the screen. In fact, the narrators started to take over from the film as the real entertainment source and the best could earn excellent salaries; naturally, the advent of talkies ended their careers. The Rokku district was also the site of the first high-rise building which was destroyed in the 1923 earthquake.

Asakusa also has several **Kabuki** theatres in the main streets on the eastern side of the temple complex. These theatres are frequented by the local residents and are not the ones to be found along the normal tourist 'trail'.

*Arakawa line, Ikebukuro*

As in any part of the world it is the people who provide the true atmosphere. Because of the popularity of the Asakusa Kannon temple you can see the different facets of Japanese society from the young who look on a visit as a 'day out' but the adults adopt a more devout approach. There are the wonderful 'characters' to be found tending their tiny gardens in the crowded residences nearby; there's the elderly community 'policeman' with his armband and baton stopping for a chat with a shopkeeper; there's the woman shoe-cleaner in a small arcade sitting with head demurely bowed waiting for the rare customer. People-watching is as interesting as touring the sights.

*Ganza Festival*

## Ryogoku

The Ryogoku district has an almost sacred place in Japanese life being the home base for the **sumo wrestlers**. On the eastern side of the Sumida river, its streets tremble to the ponderous strides of these mighty Goliaths who live, work and eat (obviously!) in Ryogoku.

Ryogoku is two stops from Akihabara on the Sobu line. Next to the station, on the right hand side as you leave from the rear exit, is the massive **Kokugikan**, the 11,500 seat stadium which is Japan's top sumo wrestling forum. As the wrestlers move round the country the sport is a seasonal fixture with January, May, September and December being the months during which they perform in Tokyo. Performances are always booked out ahead although seats are kept for the tour companies who offer combined transport/performance packages for tourists (prices are expensive though). If you can't get a seat don't worry as one television channel covers all the events throughout the day.

The wrestlers are a common sight on the streets of Ryogoku as they huff, puff and sweat their way in their **yukata** (kimono) between bouts or to the restaurants which cater for their special 'dietary' needs with dishes such as their basic staple of life, chanko, a stew of chicken, fish and vegetables. It is interesting to note they will rarely eat red meat as it comes from an animal with four feet and to be on '*four feet*' in sumo wrestling terms means defeat.

The young wrestlers learning their trade are attached to

individual 'stables' controlled by a retired, former master wrestler. Like the system of 'fagging' in English public schools, they perform all the fetch-and-carry duties for the senior wrestlers while being trained in the fine art of the sport, although the term 'fine art' may seem a little strange to the foreign onlooker who is often both bemused and amused at the sight of all that flab bouncing around the ring. However the top sumo wrestlers are heroes and fans can be seen hanging around the entrance to the stadium hoping for a glimpse of their favourite, or else, walking along the main street trying to fit their hands into the concrete outlines on the front of the memorials to the great wrestlers which line the street like a Japanese version of Hollywood's Walk of Fame.

Naturally the big interest for visitors to the Ryogoku district is to see the '**Mammoths of the Mat**'. Yet there are two other sights well worth considering there. Both deal with death. One is of a tragic nature. The other has a slight twist.

After seeing the **Kokugikan** (Sumo Stadium) return to the Ryogoku station and walk east towards the rear of the station until you come to the next main road. Then head north again...in other words along the rear of the stadium for several blocks. This will bring you to the **Earthquake Memorial Museum and Cenotaph**

On Sept.1, 1923, just before noon, Nature hit Tokyo with one of her most devastating weapons.....earthquake. This was to extend through the central district and as far as Yokohama. In Ryogoku a block land remained vacant waiting for the erection of a new school. When the first tremor hit, the local residents fled their homes and congregated on this land which seemed less vulnerable due to the lack of buildings or trees. However the fires that followed in the wake of the earthquake swept in huge balls of flame across the site killing all those huddled there for safety. Estimates of the death toll range from 28,000 to 40,000.

A whole block is now occupied by the Museum and Cenotaph which are set amidst parklands.

The Museum is a drab, brick building with equally drab interiors. However it does contain a collection of photographs which manage to convey the horror of this tragedy. There are also various charred remnants including fragments of books, bottles and even an antique typewriter. Along the walls are large paintings in the 'heroic' mould showing the Emperor visiting the ruined areas. Outside there are the blackened, rusting skeletons of old machinery. There is also a small, poignant statue showing several kiddies, a tribute to the 5,000 children who died here.

*Suiteng Shrine*

The Cenotaph is built in traditional three-storey style. A tall central chamber for prayer and meditation is lined by rather lurid and dramatic paintings of the earthquake. Below the Cenotaph in basement rooms not open to the public are the remains of some 50,000 people who died either in the earthquake or during the bombing of World War II.

If you leave the Memorial Museum by the rear, west gate the next block will bring you to the main road running along the front of the Sumo Stadium. Head south again past the stadium, under the railway bridge and keep on until the street ends at the T-junction with Ryogoku 2-Chome, the main thoroughfare of Ryogoku.

At the T-junction you will see a typical temple archway. This leads to the temple of **Ekoin**. Although it originally was intended for prayers for those who died unidentified following a tradition started with the Fire of 1657 when 100,000 people perished, in recent years it has become a temple and cemetery for pets. Local residents bring their dead fido's and moggies in neatly wrapped boxes (the Japanese passion for packaging even extends to moribund mutts). After a short time in a small 'reception hall' the animal is then incinerated and the ashes put in one of a series of metal lockers in some temporary-looking buildings by the side of the temple. The lockers are often decorated with flowers and photos of the dearly departed

*Nakamise Street, Tokyo*

and the owners return regularly to pay a visit and pray. Unlike China where they delight in eating dogs, the Japanese, in line with Shinto thinking, show much more respect for all animal life. In fact, as early as 1687, the fifth Tokugawa shogun, **Tsunayoshi**, issued an edict commanding all Japanese to be kind to animals, especially dogs as Tsunayoshi had been born in the Year of the Dog. The death penalty or expulsion to remote islands was the penalty for ill-treating dogs. When the law was repealed in 1709 upon Tsunayoshi's death, 13,000 offenders were in prison for breaking its provisions.

Also in the grounds of the Ekoin temple is a monument to **Nezum Kozo** know by the name of '*Rat Boy*' for his swiftness and cunning. Nezumi Kozo was a 19th. century Japanese Robin Hood, taking from the rich to give to the poor. His real name was Jirokich who took up the life of a robber upon being disowned by his father. His exploits robbing the homes of the samurai, which led to his death by execution, inspired a kabuki drama with his role being taken by Ichikawa Dansho who, following the success of the play, erected this tomb at Ekoin. Students hoping for success in exams as well as local pickpockets and burglars wishing for a different type of good fortune pray at the tomb and chip a small piece for luck. So many small pieces have been chipped away the original tombstone has disappeared. The stone there now is especially for this purpose.

*Harajuka, Tokyo*

## Akihabara

The exit signs at Akihabara Station (two stops north of Tokyo station on the Yamanote line) quaintly direct you to '*Electric Town*'. This is as good a description as any for Akihabara which is renowned for its electrical shops.

Most of the shops, large and small, are along Chuo-dori Avenue which you will have no trouble finding for the street adds new meaning to the word 'gaudy'. Chuo-dori Avenue is blanketed in colour. Posters, banners, neons, flashing lights and placards scream slogans and prices in loud yellows and reds. Combine this visual assault with the deafening racket of stereos and television sets blaring at full volume plus a platoon of eager salesmen harashing passers-by on the pavement and you have an asylum run by the inmates. Surprisingly one inside the stores, the noise factor is still present but the high-pressure tactics used to lure you inside appear to be for nought as it can be hard to get service as most of the staff are outside on the pavement yelling like banshees.

If possible visit early in the week, for example on Mondays when the noise is down to a muted roar. By the weekends Chuo-dori Avenue is running at full crescendo which can be un-nerving and claustrophobic with the crowds and the din.

Several of the larger stores such as **Yamagiwa** have duty free departments. These departments are usually tucked away on an upper floor and would appear to be an intrusion on the general day-to-day business of the store as they are poorly decorated, poorly stocked and poorly staffed. An interesting quirk in nearly every store is the provision of up escalators only; for the return journey down one has to use stairs.It would appear once they have your money they no longer care. For duty free shopping a passport is required.

One of the more interesting shopping precincts is right by Akihabara Station in a warren of tiny stalls underneath the railway bridge. Local electronic enthusiasts love to come here to shop or browse through the wide range of electrical components, tools and kits. Cassette players, radios and tapes are sold at bargain prices and, thankfully, it is quieter here.

Turning south along Chuo-Dori Avenue there is a bridge over the **Kanda River** which is more of a canal than a fully fledged river. Immediately over the bridge a small one-way street to the west leads to the **Transportation Museum**.

Open daily except Monday.

You can't miss the building for protruding from the outside wall are the front halves of a **Shinkansen** (Bullet Train) and a steam engine. As they are actual trains and not models it is easy to think one has momentarily wandered onto the rail tracks.

Inside the Museum is the kind of collection that will enthrall transport addicts. It is small but effective with the emphasis on trains including full size steam engines cut away to reveal the inner workings, various carriages, life-like subway 'simulators' and even such esoteric items as railway sleepers, rails and wheels. There are several venerable cars, mainly American although there is an early Subaru. Prototype helicopters, plane engines, model ships and an ancient palanquin or 'sedan chair' are to be found. Incidentally the souvenirs here are of very good quality and inexpensive.

Apart from the noisy, colourful main streets, generally the Akihabara area is dominated by feature-less office blocks and warehouses. However the bland streets often contain little surprises like the small restaurants with their rice-paper partitions, dark timber facades and a clump of bamboo clinging to life amidst the noise and the traffic fumes. In a non-descript laneway one is surprised to come to a tiny shrine guarded by two small cat-like statues wearing red scarves. This is the charm of Tokyo......being able to come across unexpected sights in the most unlikely spots.

## Ueno

If Tokyo has a cultural heart then it is to be found at Ueno, a park-filled mini-metropolis within easy distance of central Tokyo (*just four stops from Tokyo station on the JNR line*).

At Ueno there is a full representation of Japanese culture including art, folk crafts and early Japanese history together with a little zoological interest as well.

The first thing to remember when alighting at Ueno station is to head for the Tokyo end of the platform, which is the rear end if arriving from Tokyo central. Otherwise there is a very good chance you will end up leaving by a wrong entrance on the other side of the station which will only get you deeper into the urban throng. Anyway you will know you are at the right exit when you see the three-metre high stuffed panda in a glass case...its an advertisement for the Ueno zoo.

From the station exit head to the right, or the west, over the busy intersection to the far side. You will know you are heading in the right direction when you see the Pachinko parlours and the sex cinemas.

You can either turn down the small alleyways here, or closer to the station you will see some steps leading up towards Ueno Park. If you take these steps and continue straight ahead when you reach the top you will soon come to a small shrine which is dedicated to the soldiers who fought in defence of the **Shogun Keiki** in a decisive battle on 4th. July 1868. Their victorious opponents were followers of the Emperor Meiji and the defeat of the Shogun's soldiers ended not only the Tokugawa Regime but also put paid to the concept of the Shogun. Close by, almost hidden amongst the trees, is the **Kyomizu Kannondo**, the first of several temples that line the hillside overlooking **Shinobazu Pond**. Late afternoon the pond seems particularly popular as office workers hurrying home pause for a few moments to contemplate the peaceful scene of placid waters, reeds and water lilies. On a small island in the lake is **Shinobazu Temple of Benten** dedicated to the Goddess of Fortune, one reason the temple receives a number of visitors.

## Ueno Zoo

Encircles part of the pond in which are embedded special sculptures on which the birds roost.

If you stay on the high ground and head north-east (just follow the paths which are sign-posted in English) you will come to the **Tokyo National Museum** which has the best collection of Japanese artifacts, paintings and archaeological discoveries.

The Museum is on the site of the main buildings of the **Kan-eiji Temple**, built in 1625. Until its destruction in 1868, the Kan-eiji was the most prestigious and powerful temple in Japan.

There are three buildings comprising the Museum complex: the *Honkan*, an imposing, classical Japanese building in the centre, housing the main works of art, costumes and indigenous crafts; the *Toyokan*, a charming, older European-style building for the archaeological collection; and the *Hyokeikan*, a dreadful modern building for the Eastern Antiquities (if time is limited you can safely leave this one out).

Built in 1937 the Museum houses 88,000 different items including 11,000 paintings, 3,300 swords and 28,000 archaeological relics. In addition there are 112,000 books and 166,000 photographs.

The main gallery, the Honkan, is certainly the most interesting. The rooms with their lovely parquet flooring are large, although not well lit for viewing the paintings. They are grouped on two floors around a magnificent staircase. Amongst the exhibits are examples of ceramics from the major periods of Japanese history, a large collection of ritual swords and ceremonial armour and head plates (some with moustaches attached), the wonderful lacquerware in which the Japanese excel and many scrolls of calligraphy. The paintings are varied and representative of the different schools of art. These include *Toshusai Sharaku's* famous portrait of the actor Ichikawa Ebizo and the Thirty Six View of Mt Fuji by *Katsushiba Hokuai*. There also several splendid 17th century 'murals' of life in early Kyoto. Splendidly detailed they occupy a set of twelve-panelled screens.

The Archaeological Gallery's rooms encircle a round atrium two storeys high. Although there is a large collection the sameness of the various ancient rocks and bones gets a bit boring to the layman. Of chief interest are the huge, 4th century iron shield and the massive ornamental tiles from an 8th. century temple.

As with most museums the non-permanent collections are changed regularly with monthly 'turn-arounds' of various paintings.

Close to the National Museum are the **National Science Museum** and the **National Museum of Western Art**.

If you walk back through Ueno Park, which is a pleasant stroll anyway, at the southern edge of the park is a smaller intimate museum and one which will probably arouse more interest. It is the **Shitamachi Museum**, a permanent display of the life of the ordinary people during the Edo period. The Shitamachi was the district below the walls of Edo Palace - it was the home of the lower classes. The

Museum, built in 1980, has full scale replicas of typical rooms, a coopersmith's workshop and a confectionery shop. Many of the items have been donated by people from the Shitamachi area. On the upper floors there is an interesting display of early tram memorabilia and various dolls.

The grounds of Ueno Park are extensive and with its lakes, zoo, fairgrounds, museums and old temples there is enough to see to occupy a whole day. Naturally it is a popular spot for picnics but there are numerous fast food stalls and restaurants for those who don't wish to bring their own. Every April crowds gather here to have cherry blossom parties to celebrate the arrival of the blossoms.

Thrifty shoppers will also find a host of bargains in the shops that line the lower-level street running between the railway station and the park. This narrow thoroughfare is called *Ameya Yokocho*.

*Tokyo University*

*Tokyo Dome Korakuen*

## Jimbocho

The Jimbocho district is a book-lovers delight. The area is dedicated to the printed word with a host of book shops and the headquarters of the major publishers being situated here.

Jimbocho can be reached along the broad Yasukuni-dori Avenue which is one of Tokyo's longest boulevards joining Ryogoku in the East with Shinjuku in the West, circling the northern border of Central Tokyo and the Imperial Palace.

The centre Jimbocho is at the intersection with Hakusan-dori Avenue where the traffic signals play the melody 'Comin' Thru the Rye' (just why this tune was selected nobody knows).

Here are rows and rows of book shops and book stalls. In most cases the stock is purely Japanese but several larger shops have a foreign language section. But don't expect bargains even with second-hand books. Prices, even on ordinary used books of no great value, will average 30% to 50% above their original new price.

As well as books there is a fine selection of prints and scrolls in several shops.

## Korakuen

Heading north for several blocks along Hakusan-dori Avenue will bring you to Suidobashi Station. On the northern side is one of Tokyo's major amusement parks, the Korakuen.

As well as the various fun rides such as the **Skyflower parachute jump** and the **Boomerang roller coaster** there is a cycling track, a skating rink and the huge **Tokyo Dome**, Japan's first covered stadium and known locally as the **Big Egg.**

What is generally overlooked is the fact the site has one of finest gardens in the city. The gardens are over 300 years old being designed in the 17th century by the emigre Chinese scholar, **Shu Shun Sui** for the Tokugawa Mitsukuni, Lord of Mito. Chinese landscape features were followed in the design including the lovely **Full Moon Bridge** which is a semi-circular bridge that takes on the aspect of a full moon when the other half is seen reflected in the water.

## Shinjuku

Towards the end of the 16th. century when the shogun **Ieyasu Tokugawa** moved his residence to Edo (now Tokyo) the township of Shinjuku was a junction stop for travellers from the west heading to the 'big smoke'. Here the horses would be changed and the visitors would bed down for the night, usually with one of the ladies of pleasure who frequented the town.

In modern-day Shinjuku the latter activity is still practised in the pink motels that rent by the hour (pink is the colour of naughtiness in Tokyo....it indicates houses of dubious fame, sex shops and porn cinemas).

As for the horses? The riders no longer change their steeds; instead they change trains, for Shinjuku Station is where nine different rail lines meet at what must be the world's busiest rail station (2 million people use the station in the morning peak and again in the evening plus the crowds that flock during the day).

For the visitor it can be pure hell. The tendency to panic when confronted with the awesome streams of people and the language barrier becomes very real.

Just finding the right exit is a problem in itself. Running the north/south length of the station for nearly a kilometre is the Metro Promenade with exits to the west and east branching off. When you do emerge you can find yourself in one of the major department stores that straddle the subway system or in a high-rise street where everything is larger than life and where everything looks terribly similar.

The west side of Shinjuku station is the more modern part with more skyscrapers than any other part of Tokyo. The fact the oldest building dates from 1971 says something about the area. This section is possibly the least interesting unless you like tall buildings. But with the hotels like the Hilton and the Century Hyatt it is a good spot to make your base with the excellent shopping, the access to the night life and the number of converging rail-lines which can link you quickly with other parts of the city. Incidentally, the Shinjuku area has long been considered the safest place in Tokyo in case of an earthquake.

The New Metropolitan Centre is considered a prototype of a future Tokyo although the masses of concrete and the dwarfing effect of the skyscrapers that make up the complex are a touch depressing. As with any modern city that continually reaches for the sky there is a dehumanising aspect about the canyons of steel and glass. Impressive? Yes. Inspiring? Doubtful.

The east side of Shinjuku station is more of a 'people' district. The buildings are of a comfortable nature and the tiny streets and thoroughfares, packed with restaurants, bars, department stores and hole-in-the-wall shops has much more allure despite the sleazy nature of some sections.

As you leave by the eastern exit of the station one of the first things you will see is **Studio Alta** with its giant video screen, nearby is another video set up - some twenty to thirty television sets are on an overhead grid all pounding out the same rock videos. The noise is quite astounding, indeed, this particular section of Shinjuku must have a decibel rate equivalent to a thousand jack-hammers. It makes Hong Kong sound like a rural outpost.

Any of the pedestrian malls, crowded with shops and shoppers, will lead you onto Shinjuku-dori Avenue which runs past the big department stores, *My City, Mitsukoshi, Marui* and *Isetan*. Like the Chuo-dori in the Ginza, Shinjuku-dori closed to traffic on Sundays to provide a wide shopping mall. Here look for the fortune-tellers who operate small sidewalk booths in the shadow of the department stores. There is always a line of people, usually women, waiting patiently for their turn with the zeichiku, the divination sticks which are shaken (not stirred) and then interpreted by the fortune teller. Palms and facial signs may also be used. It seems slightly incongruous in this sophisticated, modern city to see the old ways still being practised.

Running parallel with Shinjuku-dori is Yasukuni-dori Avenue which commences its long journey through Tokyo at Ryogoku in the East and then finally runs out of steam here by the railway yards. This is the broadest avenue in

Shinjuku and is crowded day and night. However the buildings are all of a manageable size so you don't get that overpowering feeling of claustrophobia that you do elsewhere. The area around here is noted for its discount camera stores, brightly lit establishments with colourful signs and banners and tantalising shelves jammed with the latest camera wizardry. The two most famous names are Yodobashi and Sakuraya. The prices still seem dear by foreign standards and it is noticeable that several of the shops no longer have a tax-free department for overseas visitors.

Two or three blocks to the east of the Shinjuku Prince Hotel is the **Kabukicho** entertainment district. Cinemas, kabuki theatres, discos, restaurants and bars abound here....and so do the prices. Be wary of some of the bars where a drink will need a letter of credit from your bank manager. Always check the prices before you sit down. A good indication is the number of unaccompanied young

*Harajuku Tokyo*

ladies you see. If there are a females scattered around the dim interior you can be very certain you haven't wandered into a typing pool by mistake. Further north beyond the Koma Theatre is *Ni-chome*, the gay district. The best advice is to keep to the well populated areas, watch where the average local goes for a drink and avoid bars and clubs who use touts to drum up business.

South of Shinjuku-dori Avenue and about fifteen minutes by foot from Shinjuku station, are the **Shinjuku Gyoen Gardens**. The gardens, which extend to over 150 acres, were designed for a daimyo (feudal baron) and were later incorporated into the Imperial portfolio. After World War II they became a public park. The Japanese skill in landscaping has been put to excellent use although they have utilised French and English model gardens to add variety to the lakes, lawns and man-made hills. The gardens are in marked contrast to the maelstrom of noise and people only minutes away.

*Tokyo View*

*Harajuku, Tokyo*

## Harajuku

Strictly for the young, Harajuku caters for teenage trends in fashion and food. On the eastern side of the quaint, English village style railway station, the streets drop away down a steep hill. To stand at the top on a weekend or a public holiday is to look down on a carpet of heads along Takeshita Street. Because the street is narrow there is a congestion here which can be quite magnificent. The sound of rock music pounds out from every fashion boutique and record store who believe competition in sound is essential to selling. Fast food shops and ice cream parlours are always packed. Omote-sando dori Avenue is a much broader avenue and is also popular.

Harajuku is the honey-pot for the bumble bees of punk whose outrageous hair styles are coiffured here and whose clothes come off the racks of the newest, trendiest boutique. A stop here is a prelude to crossing the railway line into Yoyogi Park.

## Yoyogi Park

Yoyogi ranks with Ueno as the largest public parks in Tokyo. However Yoyogi far outstrips Ueno in one department: it is the noisiest park in Japan, and possibly the world!

The reason is deafeningly clear. Any weekend or public holiday Tokyo's amateur rock bands gather along the avenue dividing the park proper from the **Yoyogi Sports Complex**. The kids set up their amplifiers, turn the volume to *extremely loud* and then let loose. What adds to the inferno of noise is the fact the bands all play at the same time and all with different songs. So the bedlam of ten or fifteen rock bands in merry battle has to be heard to be believed. Even if you retreat into the forests at the furthest corner of the park there is still the incessant bass thumping of the music. So the big tip is: **visit Yoyogi on a weekday**.

Yoyogi Park is noted for its **Meiji Shrine Inner Garden** (the Outer Garden is a kilometre or so to the east). At the centre of the garden is the superb **Meiji Shrine**, consecrated to the **Emperor Meiji**, great grandfather of the present Emperor. Considered the father of modern Japan, Meiji's birthday, November 3rd, is celebrated as **Culture Day** and is a national holiday.

Built in 1920 the shrine is set amidst 126,000 trees spread over 150 acres. The walk along the gravelled paths through the deep groves of trees is a pleasant experience in itself. Entrance to the temple complex is through the largest wooden archway in Japan, being 12 metres high with its top span being 17 metres wide. As with other Shinto shrines entrance to the innermost part of the temple is not allowed for the general public. If you are there at weekends you may be lucky enough to see a wedding procession led by the priest and his acolytes in traditional Shinto robes and headgear. The day NOT to be there is New Year's Day as it is considered the most important shrine at which to make the first visit for the dawning year. Up to 2,500,000 people will pay their respects on that day.

The southern end of the park is a recreation area with wide fields, picnic areas and wooded parkland where parents can relax with their youngsters.

Over the other side of the road, after negotiating the rock bands (a pedestrian bridge puts you above the noise, except, like heat, it rises) there is a major sports quarter built for the *1964 Olympic Games*. The grounds house a futuristic indoor sports stadium and swimming pool holding 15,000 spectators, basketball hall, tennis courts and soccer ovals. The forecourt of the stadium offers good views across the surrounding suburbs. On public holidays a large flea market is held in the adjacent park area.

To the rear of the sports stadium rises the 23 storey **NHK Broadcasting Centre**, the government radio and television network. With an overseas radio service operating in 21 languages together with five domestic radio and television services the centre is one of the world's busiest broadcast networks. Regular tours for the public are available but not all the guides will speak English. There is also a museum devoted to the history of the electronic media and a 4,000 seat auditorium.

## Akasaka

The name is a combination of two Japanese words: *aka 'red'*, and *saka 'slope'*. This refers to the **akane plants** which gave a red dye and grew on the hillsides here, along with tea bushes, during the Edo period.

As Akasaka developed it gradually became the haunt of high-ranking government and military officials who used to frequent the ryotei, very exclusive restaurants where they would dine and be entertained by the **geisha**, the best of whom lived and worked in Akasaka. The ryotei is still the favoured type of restaurant for the conduct of business and backroom politics at the highest level. Few ordinary Japanese ever see the inside of a ryotei let alone use its expensive services which include the elegant **Kaiseki**, a refined and subtle form of cooking that evolved with the tea ceremony.

Because of the pleasant natural surroundings the district has been popular with local businessmen and media personalities who followed in the wake of the *TBS Tele-*

*Akasaka Palace*

*vision network* who set up their headquarters here. Overseas companies also found it ideal for their offices and for executive residences as did numerous foreign embassies. This would account for the sophisticated shopping centred around Sotobori-dori Avenue (reached by either the Maranouchi or Ginza lines). In the side streets off Sotobori-dori is a web of elegant bars, high-class fashion and jewellery shops, excellent restaurants, night-clubs, cabarets and discos. The eating is particularly good here and you can dine inexpensively at a small ramen or noodle shop, eat **fugu**, 'blowfish', at a specially licensed restaurant or join the young businessmen at their favourite bar-cum-restaurant where each drinker has his own private bottle of sake or whisky in a niche in the wall. Beer lovers even have a cafe ('Winds') devoted to various types of beer and beer cocktails although the combination of beer with lemon juice, coffee, Tia Maria or anything else you care to name leaves a lot to be desired. The **Suntory Museum**, although sponsored by one of Japan's major brewing and distilling companies, is devoted to the visual arts and not mankind's thirst. Traditional Japanese paintings, lacquer ware and ceramics are on display along with regular special exhibitions. An adjacent tea house provides regular tea ceremonies.

Several blocks south along Sotobori-dori Avenue and on a small hill behind the busy street is the **Hie Jinja Shrine**, a 20th century copy of a 15th century temple which was popular during the Tokugawa Shogunate. A large festival in mid June is dedicated to those times.

Many of Tokyo's top hotels are in Akasaka including the **Akasaka Prince** whose inspired architecture makes the hotel look like a vast, crystalline shard of ice. The 40th floor restaurant gives you some of the best views of Tokyo (on a clear day you can see Mt. Fuji). Across the road is Asia's largest hotel, the 2,100 room **New Otani** which cleverly disguises its mammoth proportions with a relatively low, sprawling design and delightful gardens (from the football-ground like lobby lounge huge picture windows seem to bring the garden inside).

To the west of the New Otani are the vast grounds of the **Akasaka Palace**. Unfortunately it is not open to the public but is reserved for state guests. Built in 1908 it was designed for the *Crown Prince* by an architect with delusions of grandeur as the exterior was modelled on Buckingham Palace and the interior on Versailles. On the western flank of the Palace grounds is the **Meiji Jingu Shrine Outer Garden** (the Inner Garden is in Yoyogi park) and within a home run is the **Jingu Baseball Stadium**, a rugby ground and the 75,000 seat **National Stadium**, Japan's largest.

## Kasumigaseki

Between the eastern border of Akasaka and the western perimeter of the Imperial Palace is Kasumigaseki, the Government district.

Although well laid out with open spaces and spread over gentle hills the grey, solid buildings of bureaucracy are rather dull. If taking a city coach tour you will pass through quite rapidly, which is sufficient.

The main building of any interest is the **Diet**, the Japanese Parliament. Two large administrative wings spread out from the main central building which is topped with a pyramid-shaped roof. The building houses the chambers for the 511 members of the House of Representatives and the 252 members of the House of Councilors.

In the surrounding area you will find the Ministry of Justice, the Ministry of Foreign Affairs, the Supreme Court and the National Theatre. The latter two were both design competition winners so show a bit more imagination than the rest.

## Roppongi

The Roppongi district (on the Hibiya line) more than makes up for the dullness of Kasumigaseki. It is the liveliest night-time spot in Tokyo.

To the south of Akasaka much of Roppongi nestles in the lee of the Expressway whose traffic rumbles night and day along the elevated, overhead roadway. Not that the locals would notice with the night-time frivolities that take place here.

Actually, by day Roppongi is rather quiet, as though gathering strength for the night. So, if you are not into night-life then a daytime visit would be best.

After leaving the Roppongi station head south of the Expressway. From the station exit you will see the pink facade of **Almond** which is the central meeting place for coffee and pastries before plunging into the entertainment district. Almond is on the Corner of Roppongi-dori Avenue and Imoaraizaka. Heading in a south-west direction along the base of the Expressway you can't miss the huge television screen of Wave, the giant record store; whilst, further along, camera buffs will find something to hold their interest in the *Pentax Gallery*, a museum devoted to the history of photography sponsored by the Asahi company which makes Pentax cameras.

But really Roppongi is a night creature and sightseeing takes a back seat to enjoyment. The reason Roppongi is so popular is the cheaper prices compared to the Ginza, although you can easily leave an empty wallet behind if you set your mind to it. The bars, discos, clubs and restaurants are more fashionable and less raunchy than their counterparts at Shinjuku and cater for more sophisticated tastes whether the young, Yuppie crowd at the **Hard Rock Cafe** or the business, society and celebrity community at the flashier nightclubs.

Roppongi is also home to many embassies and this adds to the 'tone' of the district.

## Tokyo Tower

Looking not unlike the Eiffel Tower, the Tokyo Tower gives some excellent views over the vast spread of Tokyo. However prices are quite steep to travel to the different levels so the budget conscious may find cheaper alternatives such as the high-rise office buildings at Shinjuku.

The tower was opened in 1958, basically as a transmission facility for various television and radio networks. It is 333 metres high and houses observation decks, restaurants, a TV studio and an aquarium. At the base of the tower you will see a small enclosure with statues of dogs. This is a memorial to the members of a dog-sled team who went on a scientific mission to the South Pole. This respect for dogs is an interesting aspect of Japanese life.

To get to the Tokyo Tower take the Toei Mita subway line to Shiba-koen and walk back along Hibiya-dori Avenue following the park. You can either take a stroll through **Shiba Park** in the direction of the tower or continue to the northern end of the park and pay a visit to the **Zojoji Temple**. This is the chief temple of the Jodo Buddhist sect and is both large and interesting although it is not immediately noticeable from the road. If you don't wish to visit the temple then a path between the temple and the Tokyo Prince Hotel will take you to the tower. Alternatively you can take the Hibiya line to Kamiyacho station and head south. As the tower is so visible you won't get lost.

The districts of **Shiba** and **Hamamatsucho**, to the south and east of Shiba Park respectively, can provide a glimpse into ordinary suburban life in Tokyo. There are no spectacular sights but just the chance to wander along tiny streets and see the local householders go about their daily routines. Although most of the homes are of post-war construction you can still come across the odd example of an older home that escaped the bombing.

**INFOTIP:** Never make disparaging remarks on the grounds your listeners will not understand. You could be in for a rude surprise.

## Takanawa

Takanawa is not a district you would go out of your way to visit but as it is a popular place for tourist hotels (Prince Hotels have three hotels within a block of each other) Takanawa is a good example of the small experiences to be gained if you wander at will around a city and not just rely on guided coach tours.

Takanawa is dominated by a hill with the busy shopping centre around the Shinagawa station and the headquarters of the Sony Corporation at its base and the Takanawa Prince Hotel at the top (the stately, old mansion which was the original hotel is now a reception room and restaurant).

Next to the hotel on the hill, surrounded by high walls, one can glimpse the upper levels of an ancient, upper-class residence. This was formerly the home of one of the important shoguns and has been converted into a private museum by the *Ajinomoto* company.

Early morning is a good time to wander round areas like Takanawa for you share the near-empty streets with but a few joggers, the odd local walking the dog and the newspaper boys.

What is immediately noticeable is the love of plants and trees. Few of the homes have gardens but with hardly an exception each has some form of greenery whether in the form of window boxes, a clump of bamboo planted near a door, a small cypress by a fence post or vines clinging to a post.

On Sakurada-dori Avenue is the **Meiji Gakuin University** whose wooded grounds blend in Tudor style buildings with the normal featureless modern constructions common to educational facilities the world over.

Takanawa's **Fire Station** is a strange circular building not unlike a lighthouse and looks as though it has been transplanted from a British seaside resort. Next door is the *utilitarian Police Station* which looks down on a small modern temple, which, police station notwithstanding, has its own security cameras throughout the grounds.

## Kuhonbutsu

Well to the west of Tokyo, Kuhonbutsu won't be found on the normal tourist map. The fact that it is a little difficult to get to will also deter most; but, if you wish to see one of the loveliest small temples in Tokyo and nine, stunning gold Buddhas then it is worth the effort.

The easiest way to get to Kuhonbutsu is to take the Tokaido Line to Oimachi changing to the Tokyu-Oimachi Line direct to Kuhonbutsu.

*Tokyo Broadcasting Centre*

Upon leaving the tiny station turn left up the tiny street past the tiny shops....it's that kind of tiny suburb.

Within 50 metres you will come to an intersection and on the opposite, left corner is a grove of trees covering a walkway to the temple of Joshinji.

Joshinji, which is on the site of the former *Okusawa Castle*, belongs to the Jodo Buddhist religion and is a branch temple of the **Zojoji Temple** in Shiba Park. Its claim to fame are the nine gold Buddhas sculpted by the priest **Kaseki** who spent 33 years on the task.

The Buddhas are kept in three halls at the rear of the temple compound. However the doors are generally closed and you will need to press your nose against the grimy glass to see the images properly.

Just inside the main archway is a small garden to the left, called the **Heron Garden** from the days when herons used to fill the area. There is also a wonderful old **Bell Tower** but the actual temple is a well-preserved handsome building to the right of the compound.

The grounds are immaculately maintained with an enchanting, small caretaker's cottage, which looks as though it was transplanted from the countryside, in one corner. Indeed, the whole complex has a tranquil, rural atmosphere thanks to the fine trees that shade and protect the temple including large nutmeg and gingko trees.

There is also a large cemetery on the northern border full of shrubs and flowers.

The surrounding suburb looks quite new with some expensive homes hiding behind the tall walls.

Tokyo Tower

## Arakawa Line Tram

This is the last surviving tram route in Tokyo which makes a journey something of a necessity for transport buffs. However, even ordinary tourists who don't have the mania for clambering over odd forms of trains and trams and noting their numbers, will enjoy the trip on the Arakawa Line, if only for the chance to see yet another side of this vast city. It's not easy to find but the effort will be worth it.

To reach the start of the Arakawa tram service, take the Maranouchi line subway to Otemachi changing to the Tozai Line until Waseda. Use the **Waseda University** exit on the north side, turn left until you come to the intersection outside the grounds of the old University buildings and then turn right. A short walk through the alleyways that bisect the new University buildings will bring you to Shin Mejiro-dori Avenue. The tram terminus is two blocks to the left. As a landmark look for an apartment building on Shin Mejiro-dori Avenue whose strange design is immediately noticeable. The facade is done in vague rococo style with ornamental scallops and what looks like representations of seaweed for the supporting pillars. This is all done in a chocolate-coloured cement rendering. Most unusual.

Before hand, if there is time spend a few minutes walking through the campus of the *Waseda University*. It became a university in 1902 after many years as a private school. The school had been founded earlier in the 19th. century by **Count Okuma Shigenobu** the scion of an old samurai family. For many years Count Okuma had been an active politician campaigning for the introduction of the parliamentary system of government and serving as Minister of Foreign Affairs in 1867. In 1889 he lost his right leg after surviving a bomb assassination attempt. Shortly after, he left politics to concentrate on the school he had built. The University is a mixture of old buildings set amongst park-like grounds and more recent campus buildings of the no-nonsense, strictly functional type.

The cream coloured trams leave the terminus every few minutes on the journey to the end destination, Minowa, which will take about 45 to 50 minutes. A ticket machine at the entrance is divided into two sections: the upper section is for throwing in the correct change; at the side there are slots for coins that require change. The drivers do not speak English and there are no English language signs on any of the platforms along the way.

There are a limited number of seats built with the small Japanese posterior in mind. Basically the trams seemed to have been designed for standing. However they are air-conditioned.

The tram travels either down the centre of the road with the rest of the traffic or in a separate, divided zone. Most of the journey is done rail-style with isolated tracks running between the suburban homes. There are frequent stops, 29 in all.

One thing you will immediately notice is the wonderful, communal atmosphere of the tram, unlike the crowded, impersonal carriages of the subway lines. Here on the Arakawa line people have time for a chat or a smile. The line is used as a shopping link for housewives doing the daily trip to the supermarket. School children clatter on board to go on an afternoon outing. Grandfathers take their grandchildren on their first rides. Nowhere else on the vast Tokyo transport system do you get this sense of being part of a community.

The same intimate, communal spirit applies to the scenery along the route. This is strictly suburban Tokyo...the home of Mr and Mrs Average. As the tram trundles along its rails there is the continuing view of backyards and peeks into neat, tiny Japanese homes. For a few minutes the tram veers out into the busy urban streets but for the most part it is just a charming, lazy

*Meiji Shrine, Tokyo*

journey through suburbia.

The final stop is **Minowa** station, a hundred metres from the Meiji-dori Avenue. There are no special attractions here but you can spend some pleasant moments poking around the little streets festooned in greenery and bright banners. A small noodle shop will sell you a big bowl for little more than loose change. The main shopping centre is a covered walkway of modern shops, but be careful of the bike riders who cheerfully speed and swerve down the length of the 'walkway'.

Not all the tiny homes are spick and span especially along the Shin Mejiro-dori Avenue where many shop owners do their business in the front rooms of their homes. It is not uncommon to peer in and see a tangle of bikes, engines and second-hand furniture cluttering up the entrance to a traditional, raised tatami room at the back.

As an alternative to the complete tram ride back, take it for three or four stops until you see the prominent sign of the Machiya station by the tram platform. Here a subway will link you quickly with Shinjuku where you can change for other destinations.

*Harajuka Station*

## Haneda Monorail and Oi Bird Park

For novelty value you might like to ride Tokyo's monorail which covers a 13 kilometre trip from Hamamatsucho station, in busy downtown Tokyo, to **Haneda Airport**.

The train is aimed at airline passengers so there is less seating to make provision for luggage facilities. On weekends and public holidays it is packed with airport sightseers and despite a seven-minute schedule you may have to wait in the long lines for one or two trains before you get on board.

The route gives a high-rise view of Tokyo's port facilities and follows one of the Tokyo Bay inlets.

It is worth breaking the journey approximately half-way at the Ryutusenta station for the antique fair and the **Oi Bird Park**.

In this otherwise nondescript district of freight terminals is held the **Heiwajima Antiques Fair** in March, May, June, September and December. This is considered the prime antiques fair in Tokyo and it is worth watching for announcements in local papers and the weekly tourist guides. The fair spreads over one floor of an office block beside the station - you won't need directions, just follow the crowds. The dealers all have small sections of floor space in which they crowd a wonderful array of antiques and old and new trivia. Even if you don't buy it is fun just to browse. Here you will find ceremonial swords, ceramics and lacquer ware, suits of armour, wind-up gramophones, watches by the score, dolls, figurines, ornamental screens, furniture, decorative comb sets and a wide range of other curios. You will find the fair extremely crowded, particularly with foreign expatriates from local embassies and overseas firms based in Tokyo. Traditional Japanese entertainment is also provided.

The other attraction is reached by turning right at the station exit and following the main road over the bridge and under the expressway overpass. Just in front you will see what looks like a large park fronting onto a cross street. Turn right down this street and about 100 metres down on the opposite side you will see steps leading up to the Oi Bird Park. Now this is not an aviary type park. In fact, it is basically a 'hide'. At the top of the steps is a concrete rotunda and observation platform surrounded by a large wooden fence. In the fence are a series of slats with small telescopes. You can use these or your own binoculars to watch the birds beyond. There is a man-made pond and a thick forest to attract the various birds. The unusual thing is the bird sanctuary is on the outer edge of Haneda Airport and as the big jumbos boom down on their descent into the airport the birds take little notice. This is one of the few

*West District, Tokyo*

bird parks in all of Japan.

Continuing on the monorail will bring you to Haneda International Airport, a misnomer now as few international flights land here since the opening in 1978 of **Narita International Airport** 60 kilometres away. Haneda airport dates from 1931 with the current terminal building having been constructed in 1955 with a face-lift in 1970. It services all the domestic routes within Japan. There is a small shrine on the top of the terminal building otherwise it is like any other airport. However weekends bring out the locals who come to stand and watch the plane arrivals and departures.

*Hibiya Tokyo*

## OUTSIDE TOKYO

There are several day trips from Tokyo which are worth doing. These are listed below. The easiest way is to take one of the scheduled sight-seeing coach trips which can be booked at the hotel travel desk. However it is possible to make your own way which will be cheaper but not necessarily easier.

### Mt. Fuji

Most foreign tourists will want to see Mt. Fuji, the most perfectly symmetrical of mountains. Generally passengers flying into Narita International Airport will get a chance to

*Maranoutsi, Tokyo*

see the sacred mountain if the weather is clear. Otherwise it will be glimpsed from the Tokyo Tower or one of Tokyo's high-rise buildings, from the coach tour of the countryside or from the window of the **Shinkansen** ('bullet train') on its way to Osaka.

Relatively few foreigners will get to climb Mt Fuji. Yet, to the Japanese it is a sacred honour to tackle the lengthy journey up the 3780 metre-high mountain.

According to an old Japanese myth, Mt Fuji came into being in a single night. A woodsman heard a dreadful noise late one evening and on fleeing outside, thinking it was an earthquake, he saw the mountain arising from the earth amidst flames and smoke. The woodsman named the terrifying natural phenomenon Fuji or 'never dies'.

Actually the myth is not that far from reality. Theory has the mountain being formed by volcanic turmoil around 256 B.C. The mountain itself has erupted three times: 800, 864 and the most violent, the month-long eruption in from mid-December 1707 to mid-January 1708 when the ashes fell on Edo (Tokyo).

In the 16th century Fuji became the centre of a cult of worship called **Fuji-ko** which is still practised today. The sacred mountain is known by many names including Fuji-san, Fuji no yama, Narusawa no takane, Tokiwa-yama and Sennin-yama.

The major coach-tour operators have daily tours to Mt Fuji, usually in conjunction with Hakone. The drive goes up to the Fifth Station (2,400 metres). This is also the starting point for climbers.

The official climbing period is from 1st July to 31st August which is about the only time the weather is predictable. Although in the middle of summer it is still chilly on the peak and downright freezing at night. Most local climbers undergo the trip to see the sunrise. As the accommodation huts are rather sparse and nearly always crowded the general practise is to leave the Fifth station at Gogome (on the north side) or Shin Gogome (on the south side) around midnight so that the 4 - 5 hour climb will get them to the peak for sunrise. Because of the frequent clouds which wreath the peak the best views are often from one of the lower stations below the peak.

Independent travellers can make their way directly to **Gogome** with buses from Hamamatsucho and Shinjuku stations. The trip takes up to three hours and as there are only two to three scheduled services per day, changing with the seasons, it is wise to check with one of the offices of the Japan Travel Bureau before setting out. Similarly check weather conditions prior to climbing and don't undertake the climb if in poor health or with breathing problems.

## Kamakura and Hakone

The day trip to Kamakura and Hakone is on all the coach operators' schedules and is possibly the most popular of any of the tours. For those with a limited time and restricted to Tokyo it's a chance to see some of the countryside, although, in the peak times you will be doing so with half of Japan, or so it will seem.

The trip starts off down the major Expressway to Yokohama a place renowned, as the guide points out, for numerous 'hotels for couples without suitcases'. Note the strange hotel near the Yokohama turnoff shaped like a ship. complete with lifeboats.

From there it is a short trip to Kamakura, for centuries the second capital of Japan. This 10th century village has seen the advent of modern times with contemporary architecture and a main road pounding through its centre. It is noted for its old **Tsurugaoka-Hachiman** temple which you won't get to see. Instead you will be taken to the **Daibutsu Kotokuin** temple to see the **Great Image of Buddha** which was originally cast in 1252 and towers eleven metres above an open square: originally it was inside a temple which was washed away by a tidal wave in the 15th century. It is a massive bronze statue which weighs in at 500 tons and is possibly the most photographed in Japan not only because of the size but also for the wonderful expression of placid contemplation the sculptor has caught.

From Kamakura the road skirts the waters of **Sagami Bay** where you can glimpse the fishermen returning with their catches while their wives hang out seaweed to dry. The guide will also point out the McDonald's store which is the No 1 such store in Japan.

At **Odiwara** the road heads inland and up into the hills. After a lunch stop at **Kawakien**, which is a pleasant mountain village of dark-timbered Japanese inns overlooking mountains streams, then onto **Lake Hakone** (alternatively you will take your lunch at a hotel over-looking the lake). This is a very pretty spot with tall pines and birch trees surrounding the lake with the regal cone of Mt Fuji to be seen in the background. There is normally time for a cablecar ride up **Mt Komagatake** which often has snow until late in Spring. There are also the remains of an ancient highway at **Hakone**, little more than a track, with an early customs post still to be seen.

By the waterfront is a tiny cemetery dedicated to **Jizo**. You will notice small statues commemorating the death of children. In front of the statues are little heaps of stones. According to an old Japanese belief, the children, after death and prior to the final judgement, have to wait in hell.

To get to the 'other side' they must build a mountain of stones to bridge the gap. The Devil keeps kicking the stones away so the parents regularly replenish the pile of stones at the grave to help their children. Jizo is the *God of Mercy* to whom the parents pray.

Depending on the tour chosen, the return trip will be via **Owakudani**, the mountain thermal region. Here there is a break so you can wander amidst the stench of sulphur to the boiling mud pools to the continual harsh cries of the crows feeding on the scraps. They claim if you eat an egg boiled in the mud pools here you will live a year longer; eat 2 eggs you will live two years longer; but if you gulp down 4 eggs you will live for evermore (actually, the wonderful binding effect that would have would make it seem like a life sentence!).

The journey back to Tokyo will be by coach but if you pay extra you can enjoy the quick bullet train ride from Odiwara.

## Nikko

This is the most scenic of the day trips that can be done from Tokyo. History amidst stunning surroundings is the major attraction.

The journey is by the Tobu Line train called, for reasons only the Japanese understand, the 'Romance Car'. It probably refers to the sheer beauty of the trip to Nikko rather than any hanky panky that would occur on board.

Nikko's renown is its fabulous temples of which it has a proud tradition of over 1200 years. The first temple in the area was built in 766 by the Buddhist bonze **Shodo-Shonin**. Forty years later it was rebuilt on a larger scale which started a rash of temple construction. By 850 **Jihaku-Daishi** has erected 3 other major temples and 36 smaller ones. The temples grew in such size and power that by the mid 13th century over 70 villages were owned by the temples. However **Hideyoshi** put an end to this three hundred years later when he confiscated and destroyed all the temples except nine.

The year after the death of **Ieyasu**, the first Tokugawa Shogun, in 1616. his remains were transferred to a newly refurbished temple at Nikko which was destroyed by fire in 1638. A new, more magnificent shrine was built by **Masatsuma Matsudaira** who was also responsible for planting a 35 kilometre avenue of **Cryptomeria Japonica** (Japanese Cedar) of which over 1200 trees still remain. The main street through Nikko is still called Cryptomeria Avenue.

The shrine he created, the **Toshogu**, is hailed as the most magnificent in Japan and alone is worth the visit to Nikko.

Entrance is up a broad, gravelled avenue surrounded by a forest of trees with a large bell tower to one side of the avenue where a monk operates the unique style of Japanese temple bell, which is more like a drum struck by a long, solid log. Immediately ahead, up some steps, is the stunning archway, the **Yomeimon Gate** or 'Twilight Gate' because it is considered so beautiful you could look at it until twilight.

The **Toshogu temple** complex is large and ornately decorated in gilt with a myriad carvings, rich facade decorations and splendidly ornamented curved roofs. Amongst the other fine buildings is the Sacred Stable with a panel depicting the **3 Wise Monkeys** ('see no evil, hear no evil, speak no evil').

From Nikko the trip then continues by coach up into the hills via the **Irohazaka**, the name given to the 48 hairpin bends you strike on the highway, 20 ascending and 28 on the way down via a different lane of the highway. Eventually this brings you to **Lake Chuzenji** where the pine-clad hillside overlooking the still waters makes a lovely setting for the **Futarasan Shrine** whose historical exhibits are the main drawcard.

At **Chuzenji Village** there is a view down from the top of **Kegon Falls**, the tallest in Japan. Although not in the same league as the Victoria or Niagara Falls, there is a special beauty about the Kegon and its setting. In winter the plunging waters turn into icicles which make for a particularly dramatic scene.

After time to view the falls, the coach returns to Nikko for the train trip back to Tokyo.

## Tsukuba

It is unlikely the average visitor will go to Tsukuba. But, the business person could very well find a trip necessary to this town just an hour's drive from Tokyo.

Tsukuba was the site of the 1985 Expo. and was a town specifically designed as a '**Science Town**' where major scientific and electronic companies could base their operations in an environment conducive to creative thinking. In other words it is very much a boffin's paradise.

So if you find yourself billeted there for any period of time and you wish to leave the antiseptic climate behind, a very short distance away in the nearby hills is the old, original village of **Tsukuba** in the shadow of **Mt Tsukuba** with its twin peaks, one male and one female. The area is famous for its toads with an old legend claiming toad sweat to be good for ailments: scientists have since verified toad sweat contains a substance which helps in clotting blood. The old-timers claim to get a toad to sweat you put it in a box lined with mirrors and the poor creature is so mortified by its ugliness that it starts to perspire. This sweat is sometimes called 'Toady cologne'! Small pottery toads are a popular item in the local souvenir shops.

A walk through the hilly streets of the village is pleasant and will eventually lead you to a Shinto Shrine with an old temple adjoining the modern dormitories of the monks and nuns.

Hiking enthusiasts will find a number of hiking trails up in the hills.

Outside Tsukuba, near the old Expo site, take note of the restaurant which has an English-language sign with the exhortation 'Have A Naice Time'. There are rumours it is run by an old Etonian!

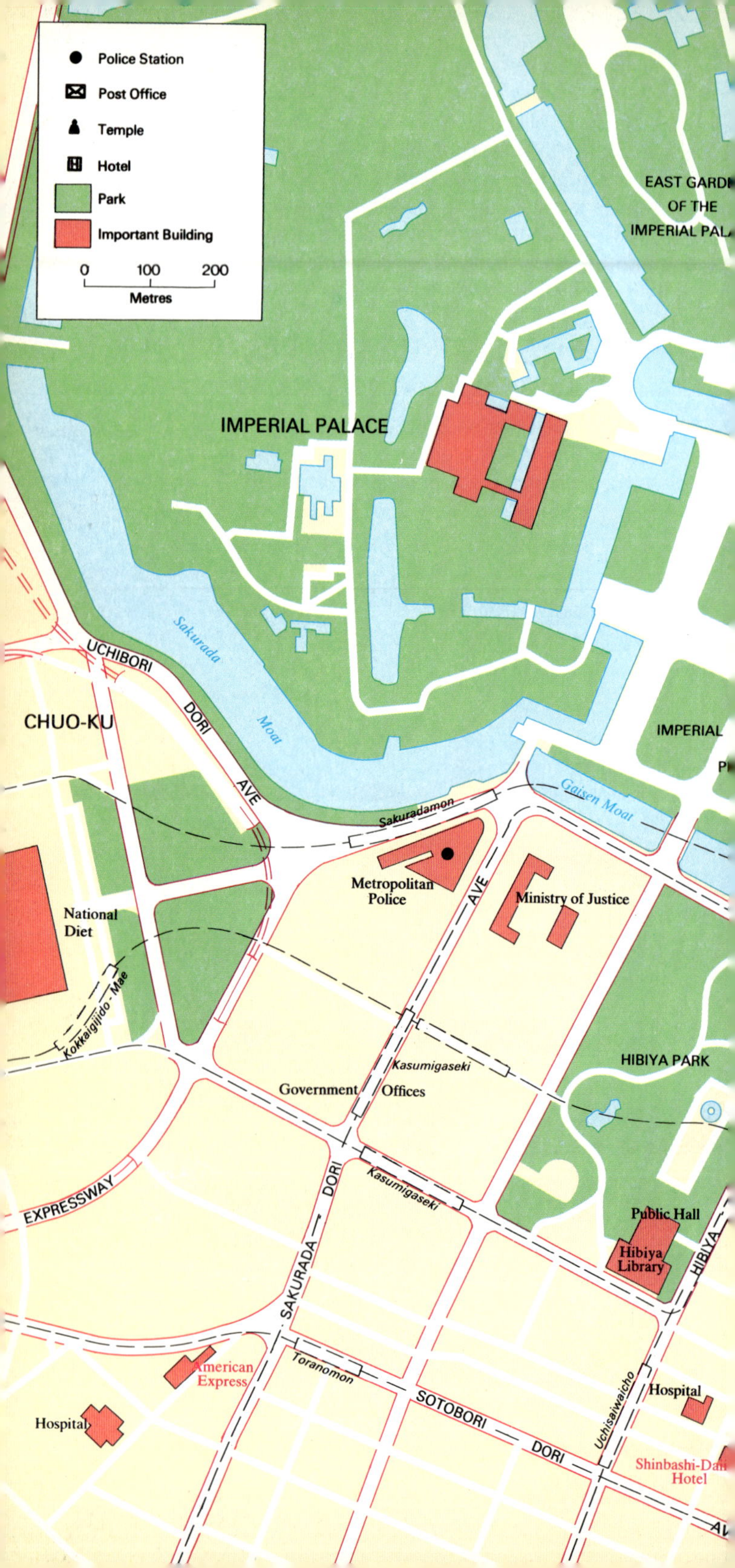

Police Station
Post Office
Temple
Hotel
Park
Important Building
0
100
200
Metres
EAST GARD
OF THE
IMPERIAL PAL
IMPERIAL PALACE
Sakurada
Moat
UCHIBORI
DORI
AVE
CHUO-KU
IMPERIAL
Gaisen Moat
Sakuradamon
Metropolitan
Police
AVE
Ministry of Justice
National
Diet
Kokkaigijido - Mae
Kasumigaseki
Government
Offices
HIBIYA PARK
EXPRESSWAY
Kasumigaseki
Public Hall
Hibiya
Library
HIBIYA
SAKURADA
DORI
American
Express
Toranomon
SOTOBORI
DORI
Uchisaiwaicho
Hospital
Hospital
Shinbashi-Dai
Hotel

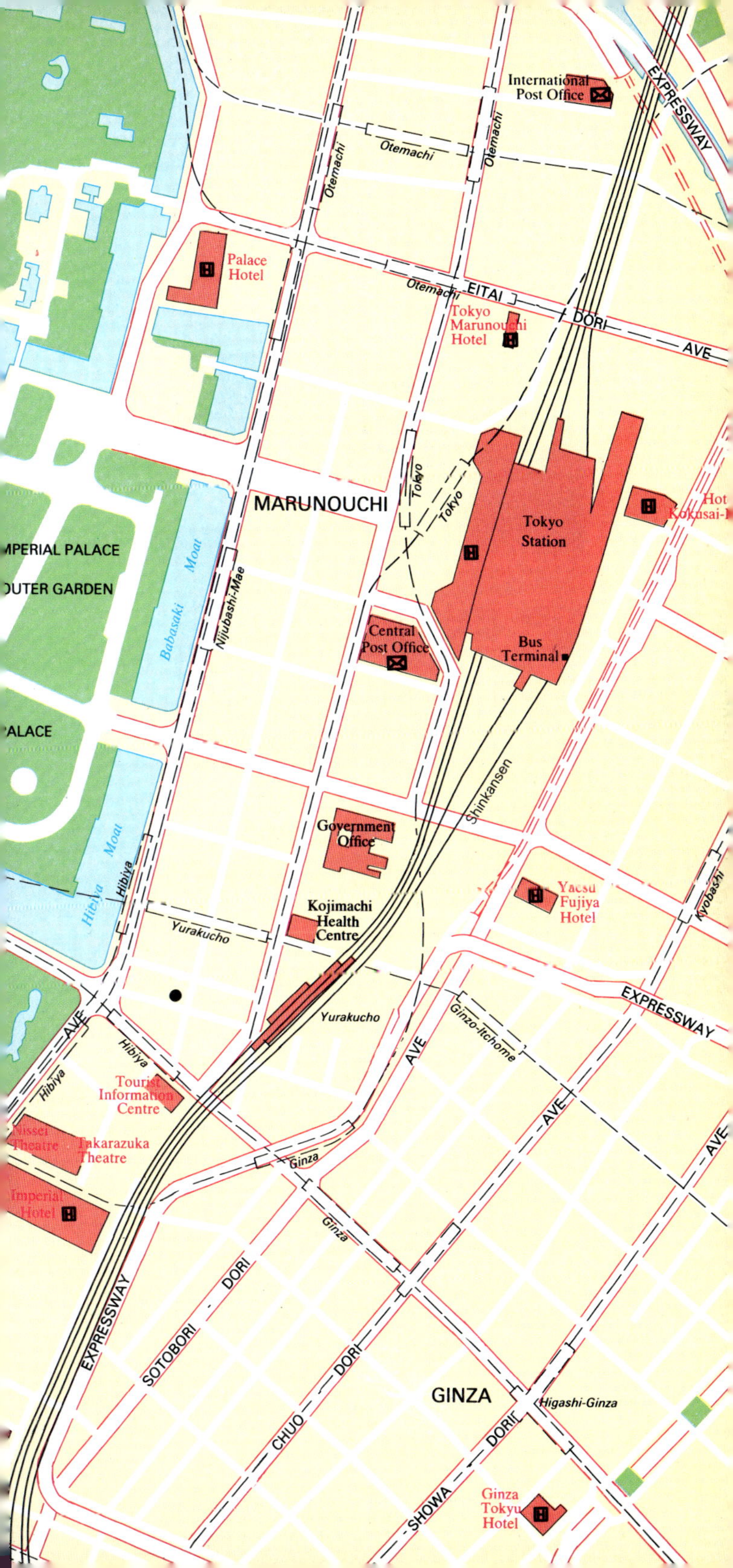
International Post Office
EXPRESSWAY
Otemachi
Otemachi
Otemachi
Palace Hotel
Otemachi
EITAI DORI AVE
Tokyo Marunouchi Hotel
Tokyo
Tokyo
MARUNOUCHI
Tokyo Station
Hot Kokusai-
IMPERIAL PALACE
OUTER GARDEN
Babasaki Moat
Nijubashi-Mae
Central Post Office
Bus Terminal
PALACE
Shinkansen
Government Office
Hibiya Moat
Hibiya
Yaesu Fujiya Hotel
Kyobashi
Kojimachi Health Centre
Yurakucho
Yurakucho
EXPRESSWAY
Ginzo-Itchome
AVE
AVE
Hibiya
Hibiya
Tourist Information Centre
AVE
AVE
Nissei Theatre
Takarazuka Theatre
Ginza
Imperial Hotel
Ginza
SOTOBORI DORI
EXPRESSWAY
CHUO DORI
GINZA
Higashi-Ginza
SHOWA DORI
Ginza Tokyu Hotel

# PART III
## Accommodation

*Akasaka Hotel*

# HOTELS

General Notes

Listing - Classification.

This third part is an up to date list of all the hotels in Japan. Hotels have been listed alphabetically within each category. They are classified as: *De Luxe, First Class and Second Class.*

Prices.

Standards of Accommodation and classifications are set by a structured authority. Check prices before departure with either pre-payment or a fixed quote.

**INFOTIP:** Get your concierge to write the hotel's name and address in Japanese. This will be of great help when getting a taxi back to the hotel.

Where given credit card abbreviations are: **AE** American Express; **V** Visa/Bankamericard; **CB** Carte Blanche; **DC** Diners; **EC** Eurocard; **CA** Master Card; and **XS** Access

**Legend**

**AC** Air Condition
**BB** -Bar
**TV** -Television/Radio
**CR** -Coference Rooms
**BS** -Sauna
**SP** -Swimming Pool
**NC** -Night Club
**CC** -Credit Cards
**BT** -Tennis

## TOKYO

### De Luxe

AKASAKA PRINCE HOTEL
Tel. 03-234-1111
1-2, Kioi-cho, Chiyoda-ku,
Tokyo 102
AC,B,R,CR,TV
CC:AE.V.DC.CA.

IMPERIAL HOTEL
Tel. 03-504-1111
1-1, Uchisaiwaicho 1-chome,
Chiyoda,Tokyo.
AC, B, R,TV,CR,S,SP.
CC:AE,V,CB,DC,EC.

KEIO PLAZA
INTERCONTINENTAL
Tel. 03-344-0111
2-1 Nishi-Shinjuku 2-chome,
Shinjuku-ku, Tokyo 160
AC,B,R,TV,CR,NC,S,SP
CC:AE,V,CB,DC,EC,CA,XS.

MIYAKO HOTEL TOKYO
Tel. 03-447-3111
1-1-50, Shiroganedai,
Minato-ku, Tokyo 108
AC,B,R,TV,CR,S.
CC:AE, V, CB, DC, EC, CA, XS.

HOTEL NEW OTANI TOKYO
Tel. 03-442-1111
4-1 Kioi-cho, Chiyoda-ku,
Tokyo 102
AC,B,R,TV,CR,S,SP,T.
CC: AE, V, CB, DC, EC, CA, XS.

NEW TAKANAWA
PRINCE HOTEL
Tel. 03-442-1111
3-13-1, Takanawa, Minato-ku,
Tokyo 108
AC,B,R,TV,CR,
CC:AE, V, CB, DC, EC, CA, XS.

OKURA
Tel. 03-582-0111
10-4, Toranomon 2-chome,
Minato-ku,Tokyo 107
AC,B,R,TV,CR,S,SP,T.
CC:AE, V, CB, DC, EC, CA.

PACIFIC MERIDIEN
Tel. 03-445-6711
3, Takanawa, Minato-ku,
Tokyo 108.
AC,B,R,TV,CR,NC,SP,S,
CC:AE, V, CB.

*Arakawa Line*

PALACE
Tel. 03-211-5211
1-1, Marunouchi 1-chome,
Chiyoda-ku,Tokyo 100.
AC,B,R,TV,CR,
CC:AE, V, CB, DC, EC, CA, XS.

TAKANAWA PRINCE
Tel. 03-447-1111
3-13-1, Takanawa,
Minato-ku,Tokyo 108.
AC,B,R,TV,CR,NC,S.
CC:AE, V, CB, DC, CA.

THE CENTURY HYATT TOKYO
Tel. 03-349-0111
2-7-2, Nishi-Shinjuku,
Shinjuku-ku,Tokyo 160.
AC,B,R,TV,CR,NC,S.
CC:AE, V, CB, DC, EC, CA, XS.

DIAMOND HOTEL
Tel. 03-263-2211
25 Ichiban-cho,
Chiyoda-ku,Tokyo
AC,B,R,TV,CR,NC,S.
CC:AE, V, CB, DC, EC, CA, XS.

TOKYO HILTON
Tel. 03-581-4511
10-3, Nagata-cho, 2-chome,
Chiyoda-ku,Tokyo 100.
AC,B,R,TV,CR,S,
CC:AE, V, CB, DC, EC, CA, XS.

TOKYO PRINCE
Tel. 03-432-1111
3-3-1, Shiba Park,
Minato-ku,Tokyo 105
AC,B,R,TV,CR,SP.
CC:AE, DC, CA.

## First Class

AOI HOTEL
Tel. 03-941-9775
13-13, Minami Otsuka
1-chome,Toshima-ku.
Tokyo

FAIRMONT HOTEL
Tel. 03-262-1151
2-1-17, Kudan Minami,
Chiyoda-ku,Tokyo
AC,B,R,TV,CR,NC,S.
CC:AE,V,CB,DC,EC,CA,XS.

GAJOEN KANKO HOTEL
Tel. 03-491-0111
1-8-1, Shimo-Meguro,
Meguro-ku,Tokyo.
AC,B,R,TV,CR,NC,S.
CC:AE,V,CB,DC,EC,CA,XS.

GINZA MARUNOUCHI
Tel. 03-543-5431
1-12, Tsukiji 4-chome,
Chuo-ku,Tokyo 104
AC,B,R,TV,CR,
CC:AE,V,CB,DC,EC,CA,XS.

GRAND PALACE
Tel. 03-264-1111
1-1,Iidabashi 1-chome
Chiyoda-ku,Tokyo 102.
AC,B,R,TV,CR,
CC:AE,V,DC,EC,CA.

HANABASHI HOTEL
Tel. 03-202-6521
370, Nishi Okubo
1-chome,
Shinjuku-ku,Tokyo

HANEDA TOKYO
Tel. 03-747-0311
8-6, Haneda-kuko
2-chome,Ota-ku
Tokyo.
AC,B,R,TV,CR,SP,
CC:AE,V,CB,DC,EC,CA,XS.

HILL-TOP HOTEL
Tel. 03-293-2311
1-1-chome,Kanada Surugada
Chiyoda-ku,Tokyo.
AC,B,R,TV,
CC: AE, V, CB.

HOTEL IBIS
Tel. 03-403-4411
14-4, Roppongi
7-chome,Minato-ku
Tokyo

HOTEL KAYU KAIKAN
Tel. 03-230-1111
8-1, Sanban-cho,
Chiyoda-ku,Tokyo

HOTEL NEW MEGURO
Tel. 03-719-8121
3-18, Chuo-cho
1-chome,Meguro-ku
Tokyo

HOTEL NEW UENO
Tel. 03-841-3221
2-5, Ueno 7-chome
Taito-ku,Tokyo

HOTEL NEW WASHINGTON
Tel. 03-460-1701
6-2, Kamiyama-cho,
Shibuya-ku,Tokyo.

HOTEL OHGAISO
Tel. 03-823-3181
3-21, Ikenohata
3-chome,
Taito-ku,Tokyo

HOTEL SEKITEI
Tel. 03-463-7191
5-45, Aobadai
3-chome,Meguro-ku
Tokyo

HOTEL SHIN-KOMATSU
Tel. 03-541-2225
9-13, Tsukiji
1-chome,Chuo-ku
Tokyo

HOTEL SUIGETSU
Tel. 03-822-4611
3-21, Ikenohata
3-chome,Taito-ku
Tokyo

HOKKE CLUB,UENO
Tel. 02-834-4131
9-19, Ueno 6-chome
Taito-ku,Tokyo.

HOLIDAY INN TOKYO
Tel. 03-553-6161
1-13-7, Hatchobori
Chuo-ku,Tokyo.
AC,B,R,TV,CR,S.
CC:AE,V,DC,EC,CA,XS.

HOTEL GRAND PALACE
Tel. 03-264-1111
1-1,Iidabashi 1-chome
Chiyoda-ku,Tokyo
AC,B,R,TV,CR,NC,S
CC:AE,V,CB,DC,EC,CA,XS.

HOTEL KOKUSAI KANKO
Tel. 03-215-3281
1-chome, Marunouchi
Chiyoda-ku,Tokyo

KASUIKAN
Tel. 03-833-1941
18-12, Yushima
3-chome
Bunkyo-ku
Tokyo

KAYABACHO PEARL HOTEL
Tel. 03-2-5, Shinkawa
1-chome,Chuo-ku
Tokyo

KEIHIN HOTEL
Tel. 03-449-5711
10-20, Takanawa
4-chome,Minato-ku
Tokyo.

KEIO PLAZA
INTER-CONTINENTAL HOTEL
Tel. 03-344-0111
2-1, Nishi-Shinjuku
2-chome,Shinjuku-ku
Tokyo.
AC,B,R,TV,
CC: AE, V, CB.

MIYAKO HOTEL TOKYO
Tel. 03-447-3111
1-50, Shiroganedai
1-chome, Minato-ku,
Tokyo.

ONOYA-ARIAKEKIEN
Tel. 03-541-2134
1-17, Tsukiji
4-chome,Chuo-ku,Tokyo.

RYOGOKU PEARL HOTEL
Tel. 03-626-3211
2-24,Yokozuna 1-chome
Sumida-ku, Tokyo.

SAN BANCHO HOTEL
Tel. 03-262-3333
1 Sanbancho Chiyoda-ku
Tokyo.

SANNO HOTEL
Tel. 03-581-6471
11-3, Nagata-cho
3-chome,Chiyoda-ku
Tokyo.

SATELLITE HOTEL
KORAKUEN
Tel. 03-814-0202
3-3,Kasuga 1-chome
Bunkyo-ku, Tokyo.

SHIBA PARK HOTEL
Tel. 03-433-4141
1-5-10,Shiba-Koen
Minato-ku,Tokyo 100.
AC,B,R,TV,CR,
CC:AE,V,DC,EC,CA,XS.

SHIBUYA TOBU HOTEL
Tel. 03-476-0111
3-1, Udagawa-cho
Shibuya-ku, Tokyo.

TAISHO CENTRAL HOTEL
Tel. 03-232-0101
27-7, Takadanobaba
1-chome, Shinjuku-ku
Tokyo.

TOKIWA HOTEL
Tel. 03-202-4321
27-9, Shinjuku
7-chome,Shinjuku-ku
Tokyo.

TOKO HOTEL
Tel. 03-494-1050
6-8, Nishi Gotanda
2-chome,Shingawa-ku
Tokyo.

TOKYO AIR-TERMINAL
Tel. 03-747-0111
2-3-1 Haneda Kuko
Ota-ku, Tokyo.
AC,B,R,TV,CR

TOKYO CITY HOTEL
Tel. 03-270-7671
9,Nihonbashi Hon-cho
1-chome,Chuo-ku,Tokyo.

TOKYO GREEN HOTEL
Tel. 03-292-3551
1-16, Misaki-cho
1-chome,Chiyoda ku,
Tokyo.

TOSHI CENTER HOTEL
Tel. 03-265-8211
4-1, Hirakawa-cho
2-chome,Chiyoda-ku
Tokyo.

TOURIST HOTEL
Tel. 03-831-0237
18-11,Higashi Ueno
3-chome,Taito-ku
Tokyo.

UENO KEISEI HOTEL
Tel. 03-833-0211
8-2,Ueno 4-chome,
Taito-ku, Tokyo.

UENO STATION HOTEL
Tel. 03-835-5111
14-23,Ueno 2-chome
Taito-ku, Tokyo.

## Second Class Hotels

ATOGOYAMA TOKYO INN
Tel. 03-431-0109
1-6 Shiba Atago-cho
Minato-ku, Tokyo 105.

GINZA DAI-ICHI
Tel. 03-542-5311
8-13-1, Ginza,
Chuo-ku, Tokyo.
AC,B,R,TV,CR.
CC: AE, DC.

SHIMBASHI DAI-ICHI
Tel. 03-501-4411
1-2-6 Shimbashi
Minato-ku, Tokyo.
AC,B,R,TV,
CC: AE, V, DC.

SHINGAWA PRINCE
Tel. 03-440-1111
4-10-30, Takanawa,
Minato-ku,Tokyo 108.
AC,B,R,TV,SP.
CC: AE, V, DC, CA.

SHINJUKU PRINCE
Tel. 03-205-1111
1-30-1,Kabuki-cho,
Shinjuku-ku,Tokyo 160.
AC,B,R,TV,
CC: AE, V, DC, CA.

TAKANAWA
Tel. 03-443-9251
2-1-17, Takanawa,
Minato-ku,Tokyo 108.
AC,B,R,TV,CR,SP.
CC: AE, V, DC.

TOKYO YMCA HOTEL
Tel. 03-293-1911
1-8,Kanada Mitoshiro-cho
Chiyoda-ku, Tokyo.

TOKYO YWCA HOSTEL
Tel. 03-293-5421
7, Kanda Surugadai
1-chome, Chiyoda-ku
Tokyo.

*Roppongi, Tokyo*

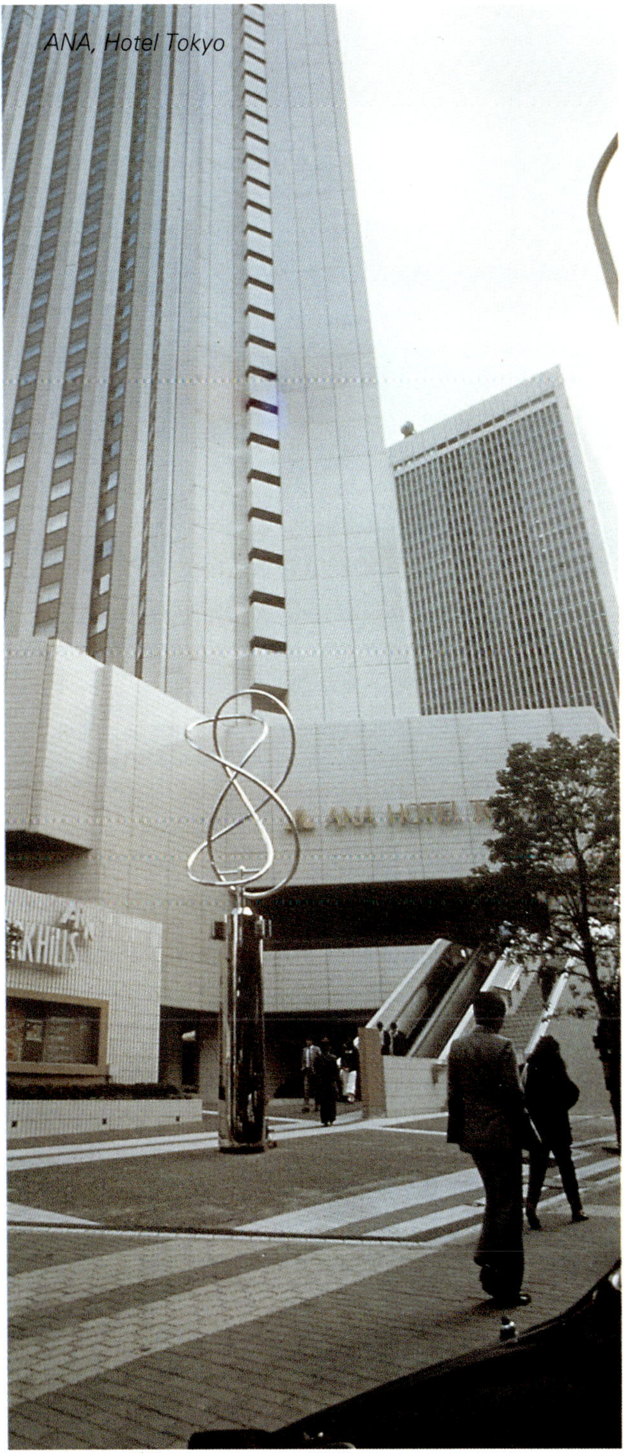

*ANA, Hotel Tokyo*

*Sumida River*

LARK

# PART IV

## Practical Information

# PRACTICAL INFORMATION

A-Z Summary

Dept. Stores, Ginza

## Advance Planning

Excellent pre-departure help can be given by your local branch of the **Japan National Tourist Organization**(JNTO). The JNTO can provide pamphlets, maps and up to date information that will be useful in planning a budget or making bookings.

### What to bring

**DOCUMENTS:** Valid passport with visa if required; insurance cards; credit cards; driver's license; student card.

**CLOTHING:** The Japanese climate will offer the extremes in weather. Tokyo has distinctive seasons with hot, humid weather in summer and freezing temperatures in winter. Although, casual clothes will be fine for travelling and sightseeing do remember the Japanese are amongst the smartest dressers in the world and any meeting that could even be slightly construed as having business overtones will require smart, business wear. Business suits for men, tailored suits or neat dresses for women. Cocktail and dinner-wear should be at least lounge suit but it would be wise to check whether dinner suit and formal gowns will be required.

Because you will be required to remove your shoes in private homes and temples, it is a good idea to pack a pair of shoes that you can slip on and off with ease. Comfortable walking shoes are always a must for sightseeing. Also check socks and stockings for cleanliness and holes.

**ODDS AND ENDS:** All consumer items are readily available in Tokyo, but you may wish to bring your own to save the time, expense and effort of looking for them: Towels, for swimming and hair; (with the exception of the larger hotels, the average Japanese hotel towel, like the bathroom itself, is designed for small bodies); extra hangers; plastic bags for wet clothes when on-the-go travelling means there is little time for using laundry facilities; a traveller's clothesline; pins; a universal bath plug. Also remember to bring extra glasses (normal prescription glasses if you wear them and sunglasses), contact lenses, medicines, prescriptions, sunscreen ointment. But don't worry unduly if you forget as fully stocked shops are always within easy reach.

**INFOTIP:** Always carry spare tissues with you. Not all public toilets have toilet paper. Also be prepared for the low Asian style toilets which involve squatting rather than sitting.

MEDICAL TIPS: Ensure you have adequate health insurance before leaving for Japan. First class Hospital and medical attention, or up to world standards, is expensive as is dental care. If on any form of medication get your doctor to write out the common name for the drug and then get that translated into Japanese at your hotel. The major hotels have their own in-house doctors; at the others a doctor can be quickly reached by ringing the front desk. If you have a pre-existing ailment that could cause unforeseen problems let the the hotel or your host know so they can be prepared in an emergency. If hard of hearing notify the front desk - this will help in case of a fire emergency when rooms need to be evacuated.

Inoculations are not required unless coming for a country with specific disease problems.

You can drink the water anywhere in Japan.

*Imperial Palace*

## Entry Regulations

Bona-fide tourists and businessmen from the following countries do not require visas for the length of stay as indicated. Travellers from all other countries do need a visa obtainable from the local Japanese consulate or embassy.

No visa required for holders of passports from the following countries for stays up to 6 (six) months for tourism or business purposes:

Austria,
West Germany,
Ireland,
Liechtenstein,
Mexico,
Switzerland,
United Kingdom.

No visa required for holders of passports from the following countries for stays up to 3 (three) months for tourism or business purposes:

Argentina,
Bahamas,
Bangladesh,
Barbados,
Belgium
Canada,
Chile,
Columbia,
Costa Rica,
Cyprus,
Denmark,
Dominican Republic,
El Salvador,
Finland,
France,
Greece,
Guatamala,
Honduras,
Iceland,
Iran,
Israel,
Italy,
Lesotho,
Luxembourg,
Malta,
Malaysia,
Mauritius,
Netherlands,
New Zealand,
Norway,
Pakistan,
Peru,
Portugal,
San Marino,
Singapore,
Spain,
Surinan,
Sweden,
Tunisia,
Turkey,
Uruguay,
Yugoslavia

No visa required for holders of passports from the following country for stays up to 14 (fourteen) months for tourism or business purposes: Brunei.

## Customs

You will be permitted to bring with you duty free:

3 bottles of alcohol; 400 cigarettes or 100 cigars or 500 grams of tobacco; 2 ounces of perfume; 2 watches or clocks; other goods to the value of 200,000 Yen.

The following items are prohibited:

Narcotics; arms and ammunition; pornography, animals; fresh fruits, vegetables and plants.

## GETTING AROUND IN TOKYO

Tokyo is made up of numerous subcenters (Marunouchi, Ginza, Asakusa, etc.), connected by ten subways, four JR commuter train lines, and private suburban networks. There is also a monorail which connects Tokyo with Haneda International Airport. Trains run every 2 to 10 minutes throughout the day and night. Tokyo is also well catered for with buses, taxis, hire cars, ferries and one tram line. The best access to this vast transportation system is a publication called **Jikokuhyo** which is a list of timetables with maps.

TRAIN: The division of the Tokyo rail service into private companies means that the purchase of tickets at stations is from separate vending machines. The ticket is purchased by price not location; and the fare is usually marked on the maps above the machines.

There are usually change machines at stations which will convert bank notes into the coinage required to purchase tickets. At many stations there are no English signs so it can be a matter of taking a guess. Don't worry though as special Fare Adjustment Offices will be at your destination or, in some cases, the fare can be adjusted by the ticket inspector who makes infrequent inspections on board the train.

**INFOTIP:** On the subway do not stare at your fellow passengers. It is considered rude.

*There is a special 'Green Ticket Counter' where you can buy tickets for the 'Shinkansen', or 'Bullet train'.*

**BUS**: Bus travel may present more of a problem for the visitor as the destinations displayed on the front of the bus are only in Japanese. Travel by bus can also be much slower than the rail service because of traffic congestion. Tickets are purchased from machines at the entrance. Most inner-city bus companies will charge a flat rate for local travel.

**FERRY**: The ferry services in Tokyo provide a very competitive form of transportation to surrounding areas. There are ferries from Tokyo to: Hokkaido; Kii-hanto peninsula; Shikoku; northern Honshu; and Okinawa.

**TAXI**: The Taxi service in Japan is similar to that of most countries. Taxis can be hailed from the curb, at designated ranks or by phone booking. An illuminated red signal in the left front window indicates a vacant vehicle. Few taxi drivers will speak English so it is necessary to have your destination written in kanji characters. Drivers will not expect a tip. Be careful of the taxi doors as they are opened and closed from inside the taxi by the driver (do not attempt to close these doors as it can ruin the mechanism and an upset Tokyo taxi driver is as ferocious as his New York counterpart).

*Akihabara, Tokyo*

## Electricity

The electric current supplied throughout Japan is 100 volts A.C with two different cycles: 50 Hz in the east and 60 Hz in the west. Separate power plugs for electric shavers are supplied in most hotels, some will provide a 220 volt outlet. Power points only accept two pin plugs. Take a set of converter plugs with you.

# ENTERTAINMENT

## Cinema

It is probably easier to see American, first release films in Tokyo than it is to see the local product. The popularity of foreign cinema in Japan means that nearly all films are subtitled rather than dubbed. A small number of theaters will offer screenings of Japanese films usually once a week. A trip to the cinema can be quite expensive; and tickets are sold as either general admission or reserved seating.

*First-run cinemas are to be found in Shinjuku, Shibuya, And the Ginza areas.*

Some of the more 'serious' specialist cinemas are:
Cine Vivant, 6-2-27 Roppongi, Minato-ku. Tel. 403-6061
Cine Saison Shibuya, 2-29-5 Dogen-zaka, Shibuya-ku. Tel. 770-1721
Haiyu-za Cinema Ten, 4-9-2 Roppongi, Minato-ku. Tel. 401-4073
Hibiya Chanter Cinema, 1-2-2 Yuraku-cho, Chiyoda-ku. Tel. 591-1511

## Performance Arts

The traditional Japanese performance arts are not easily separated into the categories of theatre, music, and dance, as often these elements co-exist with equal emphasis. For example Noh, Kabuki, and Butoh are no more theatrical events than they are solo performances of music and dance. They tend to be a combination. Noh is probably one of the most refined, if not inaccessible, of Japanese arts. Butoh represents the modern expression of traditional forms; and Kabuki is both popular and traditional.

Tokyo also plays host to a diverse range of Western entertainment, from classical music and the latest stage shows to rock concerts and jazz.

For information regarding performance dates in the arts

and in cinema one of the best English guides is **Cityscope** which can be found in the monthly publication of Tokyo Journal.

Some performance venues in Tokyo are:

Kabuki:
Kabuki-za, 4-12-15 Ginza, Chuo-ku. Tel. 541-8597.
Shimbashi Embujo, 6-18-2 Ginza, Chuo-ku. Tel. 541-2211.
National Theater of Japan, 4-1 Hayabusa, Chiyoda-ku.
Tel. 265-7411.

Noh:
Hosho Noh-gakudo, 1-5-9 Hongo. Bunkyo-ku.
Tel. 811-4843.
Kanze Noh-gakudo, 1-1-6 Shoto, Shibuya-ku.
Tel. 469-5241.
Kita Noh-gakudo, 4-6-9 Kami-Osaki, Shingawa-ku.
Tel. 491-7773.
National Noh Theater, 4-18-1 Sendagaya, Shibuya-ku.
Tel. 423-1331.
Umewaka Noh-gakuin, 2-6-14 Higashi-Nakano, Nakano-ku.
Tel. 363-7748.

## Rock and popular music

Budokan, 2-3 Kita-no-maru Koen, Chiyoda-ku.
Tel. 216-0781.
Nakano Sun Plaza, 4-1-1 Nakano, Nakano-ku.
Tel. 388-1151.

## Opera and Chamber music

Casal Hall, 1-6 Kanda Surugaqdai, Chiyoda-ku.
Tel. 294-1229.
Iino Hall, 2-1-1 Uchisaiwai-cho, Chiyoda-ku. Tel. 506-3251.
Ishibashi Memorial Hall, 4-24-24 Higashi Ueno, Taito-ku.
Tel. 843-3043.
NHK Hall, 2-2-1 Jinnan, Shibuya-ku. Tel. 465-1111.
Suntory Hall, 1-13-1 Akasaka, Minato-ku. Tel. 505-1001.
Tokyo Bunka Kaikan, 5-45 Ueno Koen, Taito-ku.
Tel. 828-2111.

# Festivals and National Holidays

The Japanese celebrate many religious and traditional festivals. There are either major national festivals or of a local nature.

## National Holidays

**Jan. 1. New Year's Day.**
The New Year's holidays are the most important celebrations in Japan. Some women will dress in traditional kimonos, and many visit shrines and hold family reunions. Streets and private houses are decorated with pine twigs, plum branches, and bamboo stalks. Families place offerings of rice cakes and flowers in their personal shrines.

**Jan. 15. Adults' Day.**
Adults' Day honors those who have reached the age of 20 years (The voting age).

**Feb. 11. National Foundation Day.**
National Foundation Day celebrates accession to the throne by the first emperor.

**Mar. 3. Doll Festival - Hina Matsuri.**
Families which have daughters celebrate this day by displaying a set of hina dolls and their accessories on tiered shelves.

*Nippon Budokan Hall*

**Mar. 20 or 21. Vernal Equinox Day.**
Celebrates the start of Spring.

**Apr. 29. Greenery Day.**

**May. 3. Constitution Memorial Day.**

**May 5. Boys Festival or Tango-no-Sekku.**
Households with boys display warrior dolls inside the house or carp shaped kites outside.

**Sept. 15. Respect for the Aged Day.**

**Sept. 23 or 24. Autumnal Equinox Day.**

**Oct. 10. Health-Sports Day.**
Commemorates the Tokyo Olympics of 1964.

**Nov. 3.**
Culture Day.

**Nov. 23.**
Labor Thanksgiving Day.

*Sub-way, Tokyo*

## Festivals in Tokyo

The following are only a few of the many festivals that are celebrated in Japan. Consult the local newspapers to check the dates of the following as the Japanese festivals tend to work on the lunar calendar.

Jan. 6.
Dezome Shiki (The Grand Parade of Tokyo's Firefighters). Celebrated by a parade of costumed firefighters along Chuo-dori avenue in the Harumi District.

Feb. Plum Blossom Festival.
The Yushima Tenjin Shrine in Bunkyo-ku hosts the plum festival from mid-Feb. to mid-March.

Feb. 3 or 4 (lunar calendar).
*Setsubun.*Setsubun marks the last day of winter. The traditional 'mamemki' ceremony is held at many of the shrines and temples; Participants throw rice and beans to drive away the evil spirits and demons.

Mar. Tulip Season.
Mar. 3 - 4. Daruma Doll Festival.
The daruma doll fair is held at the Jindaiji Temple.

Apr. Cherry Blossom Festival.
The cherry blossom time promotes one of the largest festivals on the Tokyo calendar. The month is celebrated with song and dance in the parks and in particular **Ueno** park plays host to evening cherry blossom parties.

Apr. 25 - May 5. The Annual Plant Fair.
The annual plant fair is held at the **Ikegami Honmonji Temple.**

Mid-May. Kanda Matsuri.
This festival of the Kanda Myojin Shrine features a street procession of costumed people carrying elaborate portable shrines.

Mid-May. Sanja Matsuri.
This festival takes place in Asakusa and features a procession of lion dancers.

June 10 - 16. Sanno Matsuri.
Originating in the Edo period of Tokyo, this festival of the Hie Jinja shrine in Akasaka is one of the cities major processions.

**July 13 - 16 (in the cities). Bon Festival or Bon Matsuri.**
This is a buddhist celebration in which people honor their dead relatives. This festival is held on Aug. 13 - 16 in the rural areas.

**Late July. Fireworks Festival.**
The fireworks festival takes place on the **Sumidagawa River**; it originated in the 18th century as a mass for the souls of famine victims.

**July 11 - Aug. 11.**
Ueno Park Summer Festival.

**Sept. 12 - 13. Festival of the Nogi Shrine.**
The Nogi Shrine festival is held in Akasaka.

**Oct. 11 - 13. Oeshiki.**
Oeshiki is held in honor of the death of the buddhist priest **Nichiren**, and is held at the **Ikegami Hommonji Temple**. The procession is a pilgrimage made with lighted lanterns.

**Nov. 15. 7 - 5 - 3 Festival.**
This Shinto festival honors boys who are five and girls who are seven and three.

**Dec. 14. Sengakuji Temple Festival.**
This festival is held in honor of the 47 loyal retainers who committed suicide after avenging the death of their master.

## Radio and Television.

With the exception of the United States Armed Forces Network all radio stations are Japanese-speaking, although NHK, the government station, does have several minutes of English-launguage news each day. Similarly the numerous television stations are all in the Japanese language with even foreign films and tv programmes (mainly American) dubbed. However there is a Cable Network which feeds hotels with a twenty four transmission from America's CNN news network.

Shortwave radios will pick up English language programmes from Voice of America, B.B.C. World Service, Radio Australia and Radio Moscow.

## Getting Outside of Tokyo

International flights leave from Narita International Airport, 65 kms to the east of Tokyo. There are also internal domestic flights from Narita to all major Japanese cities, but it is easier to fly from Haneda airport, 15 minutes by monorail from the heart of Tokyo. Shipping departures are from the port of Yokohama an hour by expressway from the city. Rail services offer Shinkansen (Bullet Train) express service, limited services and 'milk run' services from Tokyo to major cities on Honshu island.

# HELP!

## Consulates and Foreign Embassies

Consular activities are listed below. These services exist by agreement with the host countries and are bound by certain local regulations, as well as by orders from the home countries. Consulates are useful in answering questions regarding:

- Visas and passports
- Citizenship, dual nationality, national status
- Difficulties with local regulations (Customs, the law, etc.)
- Assistance with absentee voting in home country
- Notarization or witnessing of documents
- Assistance in case of death
- Assistance with repatriation problems

Consulates are supposed to be notified in case of hospitalization of a foreigner, if the nationality of the patient is known.

In case of arrest, your consulate should be notified. They may inform you of your rights, notify your family, register complaints and/or try to contact one of the organizations that visits prisons.

Embassy of the Argentine Republic
Chiyoda House, 17-8, Nagata-cho 2-chome
Chiyoda-ku, Tokyo
Tel. 03 (592) 0321/3

Australian Consulate-General
Osaka Kokusai Building, 2-30, Azuchi-machi,
Higashi-ku, Osaka
Tel. 06 (271) 7071/5

Embassy of the Republic of Austria
1-20, Motoazabu 1-chome,
Minato-ku, Tokyo
Tel. 03 (451) 8281

Embassy of the People's Republic of Bangladesh
7-45, Shirogane 2-chome,
Minato-ku, Tokyo
Tel. 03 (442) 1501/2

Honorary Consulate of Barbados
6 Fl, Kotobuki Building, 1-3 Yaesu 1-chome
Chuoku, Tokyo
Tel. 03 (278) 0045/6

Embassy of the Kingdom of Belgium
5, Niban-cho, Chiyoda-ku, Tokyo
Tel. 03 (262) 0191/5

Consulate-General of Belgium
3rd Fl., Osaka Kokusai Koryu Centre, 2-6 Uehon-machi
8-chome
Tennoji-ku, Osaka
Tel. 06 (773) 5289

Embassy of the Republic of Bolivia
Rm. 804, Kowa 38 Bldg., 12-24, Nishiazabu 4-chome,
Minato-ku, Tokyo,
Tel. 03 (499)5441/2

Embassy of the Federative Republic of Brazil
11-12, Kitaaoyama 2-chome, Minato-ku, Tokyo,
Tel. 03 (404) 5211/8

**Embassy of Canada**
3-8, Akasaka 7-chome, Minato-ku, Tokyo,
Tel. 03 (408) 2101/8

**Embassy of the Central African Republic**
11-19, Seta 4-chome, Setagaya-ku, Tokyo,
Tel. 03 (707) 5061/2

**Embassy of the Rep.of Chile**
8Fl., Nihonseimei Akabanebashi Bldg., 1-14, Shiba 3-chome, Minato-ku, Tokyo,
Tel. 03 (452) 7561/2,7585

**Embassy of the Peoples Rep. of China**
4-33, Motoazabi 3-chome, Minato-ku, Tokyo,
Tel. 03 (403) 3380

**Embassy of the Republic of Colombia**
10-53, Kamiosaki 3-chome, Shingawa-ku, Tokyo,
Tel. 03 (440) 6451

**Hon. Consulate Gen.of Cyprus**
Nissan Bldg., Annex, 16-19, Ginza 6-chome, Chuo-ku, Tokyo,
Tel. 03 (543) 5523

**Royal Danish Embassy**
29-6, Sarugaku-cho, Shibuya-ku, Tokyo,
Tel. 03 (496) 3001

**Embassy of the Arab Rep. of Egypt**
5-4 Aobadia 1-chome, Meguro-ku, Tokyo,
Tel. 03 (770) 8021/2

**Embassy of the Fed. Rep. of Germany**
5-10, Minamiazabu 4-chome, Minato-ku, Tokyo,
Tel. 03 (473) 0151/7

**Embassy of Finland**
5-39, Minamiazabu 3-chome, Minato-ku, Tokyo,
Tel. 03 (442) 2231

**French Embassy**
11-44, Minamiazabu 4-chome, Minato-ku, Tokyo,
Tel. 03 (473) 0171/9

**Embassy of the German Dem. Republic**
Akasaka Mansion, 5-16, Akasaka 7-chome, Minato-ku, Tokyo,
Tel. 03 (585) 5401/7

**Embassy of Greece**
16-30, Nishiazabu 3-chome, Minato-ku, Tokyo,
Tel. 03 (403) 0871

**Embassy of India**
2-11, Kudan-Minami 2-chome, Chiyoda-ku, Tokyo,
Tel. 03 (262) 2391/7

**Embassy of the Islamic Rep. of Iran**
10-32, Minamiazabu 3-chome, Minato-ku, Tokyo,
Tel. 03 (446) 8011

**Embassy of Ireland**
Kowa 25 Bldg., 8-7 Sanban-cho, Chiyoda-ku, Tokyo,
Tel. 03 (285) 7723

**Embassy of Israel**
3, Niban-cho, Chiyoda-ku, Tokyo,
Tel. 03 (264) 0911/6

**Embassy of Italy**
5-4, Mita 2-chome, Minato-ku, Tokyo,
Tel. 03 (453) 5291/6

**Embassy of the Grand Duchy of Luxemburg**
Nibancho T.S. Bldg., 2-1, Niban-cho, Chiyoda-ku, Tokyo,
Tel. 03 (265) 9621

*Setsunbun or Beam Trow*

**Philippine Consulate-General**
4Fl., Taiwa Bldg., 18-1, Akashi-cho, Chuo-ku, Kobe,
Tel. 078 (331) 9471/3

**Embassy of Portugal**
Rm. 306, Olympia Annex Apt.,
31-21, Jingumae 6-chome, Shibuya-ku,
Tokyo,
Tel. 03 (400) 7907

**Royal Embassy of Saudi Arabia**
1-53, Nagasaka-cho, Azabu, Minato-ku, Tokyo,
Tel. 03 (589) 5241/4

**Embassy of the Republic of Singapore**
12-3, Roppongi 5-chome, Minato-ku, Tokyo,
Tel. 03 (586) 9111/4

**Embassy of Spain**
3-29, Roppongi 1-chome, Minato-ku, Tokyo,
Tel. 03 (583) 8531, 8529

**Royal Swedish Embassy**
10-31, Roppongi 1-chome, Minato-ku, Tokyo,
Tel. 03 (582) 6981/9

**Embassy of Switzerland**
9-12, Minamiazabu 5-chome, Minato-ku, Tokyo,
Tel. 03 (473) 0121/3

**Royal Thai Embassy**
14-6, Kamiosaka 3-chome, Shinagawa-ku, Tokyo,
Tel. 03 (441) 7352, (442) 6750

**Embassy of the Rep. of Turkey**
33-6, Jingumae 2-chome, Shibuye-ku, Tokyo,
Tel. 03 (470) 5131/4

**United Kingdom of Great Britain**
1, Ichiban-cho, Chiyoda-ku, Tokyo,
Tel. 03 (265) 5511

**British Consulate General**
Hongkong and Shanghai Bank Bldg.,
Awaji-machi 4-chome, Higashi-ku, Osaka,
Tel. 06 (231) 3355/7

**Embassy of the United States of America**
10-5, Akasaka 1-chome, Minato-ku, Tokyo,
Tel. 03 (583) 7141

*Yushina Shrine, Tokyo*

Embassy of Malaysia
20-16, Nampeidai-machi, Shibuya-ku, Tokyo,
Tel. 03 (770) 9331/5

Embassy of the United Mexican States
15-1, Nagata-cho 2-chome, Chiyoda-ku, Tokyo,
Tel. 03 (581) 1131/5

Royal Netherlands Embassy
6-3, Shibakoen 3-chome, Minato-ku, Tokyo,
Tel. 03 (431) 5126/9

New Zealand
20-40, Kamiyama-cho, Shibuya-ku, Tokyo,
Tel. 03 (467) 2271/5

Royal Norwegian Embassy
12-2, Minamiazabu 5-chome, Minato-ku, Tokyo,
Tel. 03 (440) 2611

Embassy of the Islamic Rep. of Pakistan
14-9, Motoazabu 2-chome, Minato-ku, Tokyo,
Tel. 03 (454) 4861/4

## Medical Emergencies

Japan's medical services are of a high standard but the bills can be expensive so it is recommended that visitors obtain a medical insurance policy before departure.

**English Speaking Doctors & Hospitals in Tokyo:**

ST. LUKE'S INTERNATIONAL HOSPITAL (SEIBO BYOIN).
10, Akashicho, 1-chome, Chuo-ku, Tokyo.
Tel. 541-5151.

INTERNATIONAL CATHOLIC HOSPITAL (SEIBO BYOIN).
5-1, Naka-Ochia 2-chome, Shinju-ku, Tokyo.
Tel. 951-1111.

TOKYO SANITARIUM HOSPITAL (TOKYO EISA BYOIN).
17-3, Amanuma, 3-chome, Suginami-ku, Tokyo.
Tel. 392-6151.

JAPAN RED CROSS MEDICAL CENTER ( NIHON SEKIJUJI-SHA IRYO CENTER).
1-22, Hiroo 3 chome, Shibuya-ku, Tokyo.
Tel. 400-1311.

**Clinics & Practitioners:**

TOKYO MEDICAL AND SURGICAL CLINIC.
32 Mori Bldg., 4-30, Shiba-Koen 3-chome, Minato-ku, Tokyo.
Tel. 436-3028.

INTERNATIONAL CLINIC.
5-9, Azabudai 1-chome, Minato-ku, Tokyo.
Tel. 582-2646.

ISHAKAWA CLINIC.
Azubu Sakurada Heights, Rm. 201, 2-7, Nishi-Azubu 3-chome,
Minato-ku, Tokyo.
Tel. 401-6340.

PLESSNER'S OFFICE.
International Azabu Supermarket Bldg., 5th floor, 5-2, Minami-Azabu 4-chome, Minatu-ku, Tokyo.
Tel. 473-2057.

KING'S CLINIC.
4th floor, Olympia Annex, 31, Jingu-mae 6-chome, Shibuya-ku,
Tokyo.
Tel. 400-7917.

## Police Emergencies

Police....................Tel. 110
Fire & Ambulance..........Tel. 119

There is no charge for these calls from a public phone, however a red button must be pushed before dialing the number.

## Death

The death of a foreign citizen requires instant consultation with the appropriate Consulate by friends, relatives, hospital or police authorities.

## Lost Property or Theft

If any personal items, such as luggage, have been left at a railway station then more than likely they will still be there when you return. If not then the Station Masters office or the nearest police station (Koban) would be the first place to look. Similarly, items left in taxis will will often be returned to your hotel (if labelled) or try the Tokyo Taxi Kindaika Center Tel.648-0300. When contacting any of the above it will be necessary to find someone to assist in interpretation.

The following may help you replace your lost or stolen property. Report loss or theft immediately. Even if your property cannot be recovered, the record will be needed to replace documents, tickets, travellers' checks, or to claim insurance. You will need a police translation of your statement into English, or the language used by the issuer of your documents.

Loss or theft of ID - passports etc. should be reported to the police and to your consulate.

**Other thefts**: Go in person to the local police station. Obtain a copy of your report, making sure it has a reference number. At very least get the reference number. Make sure that you have clarified whether you have suffered a loss or theft. If possible try and take an interpreter with you.

It is suggested that you report the incident to your Consulate, as documents without resale value are often turned in.

Leave valuable items in a safe places, such as the hotel safe. Don't carry passports in obvious places - handbags or outside pockets.

## Replacement of certain items

Airline Tickets: Report the loss/theft to the airline and request replacement. A copy of the police report should be presented to the airline. Replacements can usually be issued only after the complete ticket information has been provided, and verification of your lost ticket obtained from the issuing office. With youth fare tickets you will probably have to buy a new ticket and obtain refund at the issuing office.

Credit Cards: Report loss immediately to the credit card company.All the major credit card companies, American Express, Diners Club, Visa, Mastercard, Eurocard etc. are represented in Tokyo and are listed in the local phone book.

Driving Licenses: Consult your Consulate for advice.

*Kappabashi, Tokyo*

Railway Tickets: The Railways may be able to issue replacement if the number of the lost pass can be confirmed with the issuing office (so keep a record).

Passport: Report immediately to your consulate within working hours.

Student Cards: Contact the International Youth Travel Service. You must have a valid university or college ID card.

Travellers' Checks: Issuing firms normally replace these. Depending on what proof (serial numbers, receipts from purchases, etc.) you can offer, the time of replacement varies.

At least in Tokyo you have an excellent chance of getting lost property returned as honesty is one of the prime Japanese traits.

*Ueno, Shopping Street*

## Crime

Western visitors used to looking over their shoulder in major American and English cities will find it hard to come to terms with Tokyo where there is little street crime and muggings are practically unheard of. However in some crowded areas pickpockets are active and it is not wise to flaunt wads of cash or expensive jewellery.

Of course there is crime and business and political corruption within Japan. However it does not spread onto the streets. A tourist is most unlikely to be involved in the violent struggles between the Yakuza, the organised crime gangs of Japan who control much of the sex and pornography business.

## Motoring

Traffic moves along the left hand side of the road. Driving conditions in Tokyo are adequate with the main problem being the almost constant traffic congestion. To add to this the speed limits are very low (60 km/h is the top speed on highways). The road laws are strictly enforced. Road signs are written in Kanji so it is necessary to memorise the characters of relevant destinations and turn offs. This is slowly changing as more signs are being written in Romanised language.

*Roppongi, Tokyo*

It is possible to use a domestic driving licence (from the country of origin) or an International Driving Permit for the first six months of your stay. If you intend staying for a period longer than six months then the authorities at the Shikenjo (licence office) will be able to help you obtain a Japanese driving licence.

If you wish to ride a motorcycle then you will only be aloud to ride a bike up to 400cc on a foreign licence; to ride a larger bike will require a 'riding skill test' for a Japanese licence.

## Private Cars

For a visitor to bring a car in it is necessary to have a carnet de passage en douane from an Automobile Association of the country of origin. Further information can be obtained from JAL.

## Rental Cars

Some rental car agencies in Tokyo are:
Nippon (Hertz)............................Tel. 496-0919
Toyota....................................Tel. 264-2834
Japaren...................................Tel. 352-7635
Mitsubishi Rent-a-Car.....................Tel. 294-4871
Nissan Rent-a-Car.........................Tel. 584-2341
ACU Rent-a-Car............................Tel. 364-2211

## In Case of Accident

Stop and move only if necessary.
Police....................Tel. 110
Ambulance..........Tel. 119

Call police (and ambulance if required). Exchange names and addresses, and get those of witnesses. Make sure that you get the license number of other car(s), and the name of the insurance company. Report the accident as soon as possible to your insurance company. Parties to accidents are sometimes held at police stations. Contact your consulate for advice. Say as little as possible as you may not be understood correctly.

## Traffic Laws

Cars drive, in the English manner, on the left hand side of the road. The speed limit, even on highways, is 60 km.per hour. International driving signs apply, however many directions are in Kanji characters.

## Museums

**Astromomic Museum (Goto Palace)**
21-12, Shibuya 2-chome, Shibuya-ku.Tel. 407-7409
**Azabu Museum of Art**
Excel Pavillion, 9-4, Azabu Juban 1-chome, Minato-ku.Tel. 582-1410
**Baseball Hall of Fame & Museum**
3-61, Koraku 1-chome, Bunkyo-ku.Tel. 811-3600
**Bridgestone Museum of Art**
10-1, Kyobashi 1-chome, Chuo-ku.Tel. 563-0241
**Broadcast Museum**
1-1, Atago 2-chome, Minato-ku.Tel. 433-5211
**Communications Museum**
3-1, Ohte-machi 2-chome, Chiyoda-ku.Tel. 244-6811
**Goto Art Museum**
9-25, Kaminoge 3-chome, Setagaya-ku.Tel. 703-0661
**Idemitsu Museum of Arts**
1-1, Marunouchi 3-chome, Chiyoda-ku.Tel. 213-9402
Japan Science Foundation
2-1, Kitanomaru Koen, Chiyoda-ku.Tel. 212-8471
**International Leisure Corporation**
Tokyo Tower Bldg.
2-8, Shiba-koen 4-chome, Minato-ku.Tel. 436-6661
**Japan Folkcrafts Museum**
3-33, Komaba 4-chome, Meguro-ku.Tel. 467-4527
**Meiji Shrine Homotsuden**
1-1, Yoyogi Kamizono-cho, Shibuya-ku.Tel. 379-5511
**Meiji Memorial Picture Gallery**
9, Kasumigaoka, Shinjuku-ku.Tel. 401-5179
**Museum of Maritime Science**
3-1, Higashi Yashio, Shinagawa-ku.Tel. 528-1111
**Museum of Modern Japanese Literature**
3-55, Komaba 4-chome, Megura-ku.Tel. 468-4181
**National Museum of Western Art, The**
7-7, Ueno Koen, Taito-ku.Tel. 822-0111
**Nezu Institute of Fine Art**
5-36, Minami Aoyama 6-chome, Minato-ku.Tel. 400-2536
**Okura Shukokan Museum**
10-3, Toranomo 2-chome, Minato-ku.Tel. 583-0781
**Paper Museum**
1-8, Horifune 1-chome, Kita-ku.Tel. 911-3545
**Petroleum Communication Center**
11-2, Nagata-cho 2-chome, Chiyoda-ku.Tel. 593-6495
**Riccar Art Museum**
2-3, Ginza 6-chome, Chuo-ku.Tel. 571-3254
**Sunshine Planetarium**
World Import Mart Bldg. 10th Fl.
1, Higashi Ikebukuro 1-chome, Toshima-ku.
Tel. 989-3466

**Suntory Museum of Art**
Tokyo Suntory Bldg.
2-3, Moto Akasaka 1-chome, Minato-ku.Tel. 470-1073
**Sword Museum**
25-10, Yoyogi 4-chome, Shibuya-ku.Tel. 379-1386
**Telecommunications Science Hall**
2-2, Ohte-machi 2-chome, Chiyoda-ku.Tel. 241-8080
**Tepco Electric Energy Museum**
12-10, Jinnan 1-chome, Shibuya-ku.Tel. 477-1191
**Tokyo Mertropolitan Art Museum**
8-36, Ueno Koen, Taito-ku.Tel. 823-6921
**Tokyo National Museum**
13-9, Ueno Koen, Taito-ku.Tel. 822-1111
**Transportation Museum**
1-25, Kanda Suda-cho, Chiyoda-ku.Tel. 251-8481
**Yamatane Museum of Art**
7-12, Nihonbashi Kabuto-cho, Chuo-ku.Tel. 669-4056

*Ganza Festival*

## Post

Japan's postal service along with telephone and telegraphic facilites are excellent. Post offices are to be found in all districts. Tokyo Central Post Office is open 24 hours except Sundays and public holidays.

The service is convenient for tourists as they keep quite long hours: local offices are open from 9am - 5pm; main district offices are open from 8am - 7pm; and the central post office in Tokyo is open 24 hours a day. It is not necessary to address letters with kanji characters (this applies for both incoming and outgoing mail). There is a special post office in Tokyo for overseas mail and this is known as the Tokyo International Post Office; information in English is available here.

## Poste Restante

Travelers can have post addressed to Poste Restante at any of Japans post offices. This mail is held for 30 days then returned to sender. When receiving this mail present your identification and ask for 'tome oki' or 'kyoku dome'. American Express and some embassies will also hold mail.

*Harajuku, Tokyo*

## Restaurants & Nightlife

Tokyo has a greater diversity and choice of eateries and entertainment venues than any other Japanese city. The visitor can find outings a little daunting if unescorted because it is not often apparent what sort of budget a particular establishment caters for; and whether or not the employees speak English.

### Food

Tokyo has many specialist restaurants, both Japanese and foreign. The institution of the business entertainment expense account, and the fact that most Japanese prefer not to entertain guests at home, has resulted in 190,000 bars and restaurants in the Tokyo area. The standard of cooking and sanitation is uniformly high from the very expensive to the very modest establishments.

> **INFOTIP:** Tipping is not required. However it is becoming customary for restaurants to add a 10% service charge to the bill.

Japanese cuisine depends on a balance of delicate and simple flavours; rice, fish, vegetables, and soy bean products are the most common ingredients. Presentation is all important and an average meal will usually consist of three or four dishes which are served at the same time. Traditionally deserts are not a feature of the Japanese menu, however some of the more Western style restaurants may provide them.

> **INFOTIP:** At a Japanese meal do not pour your own drinks. Let your neighbour do that...and vice versa.

Some common dishes you will find on the Japanese menu are:

**Sashimi**: a variety of prepared raw fish.
**Sushir**: raw or cooked fish prepared with rice, vegetables and sea-weed.
**Tempura**: vegetables coated in batter and deep-fried.
**Sukiyaki**: a sake and soy broth containing tofu, noodles, thinly sliced beef and vegetables. Variations on this dish are Shabu-shabu and Jingis Khan.
**Domburi**: a chicken, egg, meat and rice dish.
**Okonomiyaki**: seafood incorporated into a pancake style batter.

## Restaurants

The following is a list of some of Tokyo's inexpensive to moderately priced restaurants with English speaking staff:

> **INFOTIP:** If taken out by a Japanese host for drinks and/or a meal you may have to 'sing for your supper'. It is customary in many night spots for the patrons and their guests to get up and sing or recite. Learn a couple of songs, just in case.

Go-nin Hyakuho.
3-10-3 Roppongi, Minato. Tel. 470-1675.
Credit cards: AE, DC, MC, V.
No reservations. Open 11.30am-10pm.

Inakaya.
6-8-23 Roppongi, Minato-ku. Tel. 478-0092.
No credit cards. No reservations required.
Open 6pm-3am.

Takeno.
6-21-2 Tsukiji, Chuo-ku. Tel. 541-8691.
No credit cards. No reservations.
Open 11am-8.30pm.

Tatsumiya.
1-33-5 Asakusa, Taito-ku. Tel. 842-7373.
No credit cards. Reservations required.
Open 12-2pm and 5-9pm, closed on Monday.

Tonki.
1-1-2 Shimo-Meguro, Meguro-ku. Tel. 491-9928.
Credit cards: DC, V.
No reservations required. Open 4-10.45pm.

## Nightspots

The following lists of nightspots are those which have English speaking employees.

Bars and Beer Halls:

Garbus Cine Cafe. 1-2-2 Yurakucho, Chiyoda-ku.
Tel. 501-3185.
The Glasshopper. Tamachi-dori Ave., Akasaka, Minato-ku.
Tel. 586-3579.

Hard Rock Cafe. 5-4-20 Roppongi, Minato-ku.
Tel. 408-7018.

Henry Africa. 3-13-14 Akasaka, Minato-ku.
Tel. 585-0149.

Highlander. Hotel Okura, 2-10-4 Toranomon, Minato-ku. Tel. 582-0111.

Ikka. 6-3-5 Ginza, Chuo-ku. Tel. 574-1819.

Ishikawa Haragura. 2-2-2 Ginza, B1, Chuo-ku.
Tel. 561-2650.

Ivy House. 2-2-2 Ginza, Chuo-ku. Tel. 561-2650.

Kirin City. Izumo Bldg., 8-8, Ginza, Chuo-ku.
Tel. 571-7739.

Levante Beer Hall. 2-8-7 Yurakucho, Chiyoda-ku.
Tel. 201-2661.

Maggie's Revenge. 3-8-12 Roppongi, Minato-ku.
Tel. 479-1096.

The Old Imperial Bar. Imperial Hotel, 1-1-1 Uchisaiwaicho, Chiyoda-ku. Tel. 504-1111.

Paradiso. 3-13-12 Roppongi, Minato-ku. Tel. 478-4212.

Sapporo Lion. 6-10-12 Ginza, Chuo-ku. Tel. 572-2291.

Suishin. 7-2-15 Ginza. Tel. 214-8046.

Wine Bar. 52-16-5 Roppongi, Minato-ku. Tel. 504-5790.

**Nightclubs, Discos, and Live Music Venues** :

Akasaka Mugen. 3-8-17 Akasaka Minato-ku. Tel. 584-4481.

Byblos. 8-17 Akasaka 3-chome, Minato-ku. Tel. 584-4484.

Chaps. 3-14-8 Roppongi, Minato-ku. Tel. 479-2136.

Cleo Paradiso. 3-18-2 Roppongi, Minato-ku. Tel. 586-8494.

Cordon Bleu. 6-6-4 Akasaka, Minato-ku. Tel. 582-7800.

Furusato. 3-4-1 Aobadai, Meguro-ku. Tel. 463-2310.

Last 20 Cents. 3-8-20 Roppongi, Minato-ku. Tel. 403-0091.

Lexington Queen. 3-13-14 Roppongi, Minatoku.
Tel. 401-1661.

Neo Japonesque. 5-16-5 Roppongi, Minato-ku.
Tel. 586-0050.

The New Latin Quarter. 2-13-8 Nagatacho, Chiyoda-ku.
Tel. 581-1326.

Pit Inn. 3-16-4 Shinjuku, Shinjuku-ku. Tel.254-2024.

Roppongi Pit Inn. 3-17-7 Roppongi, Minato-ku.
Tel. 585-1063.

Satin Doll. 4-9-2 Roppongi, Minato-ku. Tel.401-3080.

Showboat. Tokyo Hilton, 6-6-2 Nishi-Shinjuku, Shinjuku-ku.
Tel. 344-5111.

**INFOTIP:** The rail services close down for several hours midnight to dawn. So be prepared to take a taxi if you plan a late night.

## Shopping

The strength of the yen in recent years will mean that visitors to Japan should be constantly aware of their budget. Every-day expenses (coffee, taxi fares, admission to sporting facilities) can cost up to ten times what you would expect to pay at home. However, this should not discourage potential shopping as bargains can still be found.

**INFOTIP:** Surprisingly it is still common for Westerners to be stared at in Tokyo. Do not be embarrassed by this natural curiosity. The Japanese are particularly fascinated by the Westerners' big noses.

When travelling it is always best to buy some things, such as clothing and personal goods, at home. This pre-planning is essential when travelling to Japan. Souvenirs and Japanese items unavailable elsewhere would be the main target for shoppers as some products, such as electrical goods (stereo & video equipment, cameras etc.) are actually more expensive to buy in Japan. Remember, in ordinary shops electronic gear is designed for Japanese voltage and conditions (the line system in televsion sets for example is different to many other countries) may not be right your country. Ask first. Major electrical stores have a Tax Free section for visitors where the goods are designed for overseas use.

Prices in smaller stores and markets might be listed with Kanji instead of Arabic numerals. In such cases, just ask, 'How much?' It's a phrase that most Japanese shop-keepers will recognize, and someone will either tell you or write the price down for you. In the major department stores many of the people can speak enough English for you to complete your transaction.

Stores in Tokyo generally open around 10-11 am and close around 7-8 pm. Many stores are open daily.

Value added tax (VAT) is around 13% to 15% and is usually already included in the price. VAT exemptions are only available for goods over a certain price, and is usually posted on signs in the store. To receive a VAT exemption you must fill out forms in the store where you make your purchase.

## Where to Shop

### Akihabara

This is the place where you will see all of the very latest in Japanese electrical goods. The best deals in Japan may be found here, but generally prices are lower outside of the country.

### Aoyama

Aoyama is one of the fashion centers of Tokyo and is home to some of the leading Japanese and Western designer boutiques.

### Asakusa

Most of the shops in this area cater for tourists.

### Ginza

The Ginza is one of the major entertainment and shopping districts in Tokyo. The department stores and boutiques are exclusive and expensive.

### Harajuku

This place caters for Japanese teenagers and is therefore relatively inexpensive. Many of the small stores sell 50's and 60's clothing and kitch.

### Shibuya

This area is an entertainment district and is filled with cinemas, bars, and restaurants.

### Shinjuku

Some of Japan's most fashionable department stores are to be found here amid the gay and red light districts.

*Kabuki-Cho, Shinjuku*

## What to buy

Japan offers a wide range of unusual and interesting products, from traditional crafts to the mass-produced. The purchase of items uniquely Japanese is wise because of the high prices of imports (and common export products).

## Antiques

Antiques hold an interesting place in the everyday life of the Japanese today. Unlike the curio value that is placed upon antiques in the West, many Japanese antiques still have a functional purpose. Some antique shops to be found in Tokyo are:

Art Plaza Magatani
10-13, Toranomon, 5-chome, Minato-ku. Tel. 433-6321.
Edo Antiques
21-12, Akasaka 2-chome, Minato-ku. Tel. 584-5280.
Irori
7-4, Azabudai 1-chome, Minato-ku. Tel. 586-8105
Japan Art Center
Green Heights,
22-13, Takadanobaba 1-chome, Shinjuku. Tel. 200-5837.
Okura Oriental Art
3-14, Azabu 3-chome, Minato-ku. Tel. 585-5309.

## Bamboo and Paper Craft

Among the many traditional crafts are bamboo craft and paper craft, both of which have been produced and used by the upper class and general public alike for generations. Bamboo craft is a speciality of the Oriental countries where bamboo grows easily. Because it is so readily available, bamboo has long been used to make many of the necessities of daily life. The art of paper craft, using gaily coloured paper, has come down over the centuries as a traditional girls' handcraft.

## Ceramics

Ceramics can be difficult to transport, often they are large and very fragile, however, if you are willing to take the trouble they can provide a cherished keepsake or gift. Much of Japanese pottery is regional and the distinctive styles come from techniques that date back to the 16th century. Some of the more prominent pottery centers are: Arita in Kyushu; Mashiko, outside of Tokyo in the Tochigi Prefecture; and Kasama, in the Ibaraki Prefecture.

## Dolls

Dolls play an important part in Japanese culture; there are two festivals each year when families display the children's dolls. The making of traditional dolls is still primarily done by hand, and they are the product of skilled craftmen. The gorgeous dresses of the hinadolls and the armor of the 'doll warriors' are all handcrafted items. Kyugetsu is a shop that has been in business for over a century and is located at: 1-20-4 Yanagibashi, Taitoku.

## Electrical Goods

Japan is the most expensive place to buy Japanese goods so the best bargains are to be had at home (duty free), or in neighboring Asian countries. If however, you wish to see or purchase the very latest in electronics then you should go to the area surrounding Akihabara Station, where you will find over 200 specialist stores.

## Games

There are a variety of different kinds of games available in Japan, from traditional games to the latest in high-tech. electronics. The most popular traditional games are shogi and go. Shogi is an Oriental version of chess. Go is a game in which black and white 'go' stones are moved about on a wooden block, much like a checker board, to occupy an enemy's position. These games hold great cultural significance, and the individual game sets can be quite elaborate works of craftmanship (and expensive).

## Kimonos

One of the most well known traditional Japanese garments is the kimono. A kimono is a dress with straight lines, made from one bolt of fabric 13 metres long and 33 cm wide, and worn like a wrap-around dress which opens at in the front. The design of the kimono, in Japanese culture, is linked with gender and social status. While men's kimonos are more plain, and are differentiated according to social status, women's kimonos are classified into several groups according to age and marital status.

## Stationery

In early times the implements used for writing and painting were highly valued and carefully guarded. The brush, the ink stick, the paper and the inkstone were carefully selected and of the best quality. The inkstone was essential for making liquid ink as one rubbed the Indian ink stick and drops of water on it. Using these implements, poems and beautiful calligraphy were written and the art of painting with Indian ink was developed. This art is known as sumi-e. Some stationery stores in Tokyo are:

Itoya
7-15, Ginza 2-chome, Chuo-ku. Tel. 561-8311.
Maruzen
3-10, Nihonbashi 2-chome, Chuo-ku. Tel. 272-7211.
Bunshodo
4-12, Ginza 3-chome, Chuo-ku. Tel. 563-1511.
Kurosawa
9-2, Ginza 6-chome, Chuo-ku. Tel. 571-8441.
Tokyu Hands 5A
12-18, Udagawa-cho, Shibuya-ku. Tel. 476-5461.

## Swords

Japanese swords (which are also known as Katana) were original used as primary weapons. However, as the ways and means of fighting developed over the years, the size and function of swords changed too. Today swords are appreciated as objects of art. Japanese swords must satisfy two basic conditions: first, they must be beautiful, and second, they must be functional. It is believed that Japanese swords represent the soul of Japanese soldiers, samurai. You will not be permitted to take a real one out of the country, but there are many beautiful, non-funtional copies available.

## Woodblock Prints

One of Japan's most representative arts is the woodblock print, also known as Ukiyo-e. The woodblock print was developed in the 16th century as a form of popular, reproducable art. Excellent copies of the well known masterpieces of Utamaro, Sharaku, Hokusai and Hiroshiga are now made using high quality printing techniques and are available at reasonable prices.

*Shibuya, Tokyo*

Iidabashi, Tokyo

## Sports & Athletics

Sumo wrestling and baseball are the two most popular spectator sports in Japan. Admission can be expensive, however both provide an excellent opportunity to see the Japanese sport-going-public in action. Sumo events are held in Tokyo: early January; early may; and mid-September.

Visitors who wish to make use of exercise facilities during there stay in Tokyo will find that the large hotels provide the most accessible fitness centers. The location of these hotels and some of their facilities are:

CENTURY HYATT, 2-7-2 Nishi-Shinjuku, Shinjuku-ku.
Tel. 349-0111.
Separate gymnasiums for men and women; and an Olympic pool.

HOTEL NEW OTANI AND TOWER, 4-1 Kioi-cho, Chiyoda-ku.
Tel. 265-1111. Private health club; four tennis courts; a golf driving range; and Olympic pool.

HOTEL OKURA, 10-4 Toranomon 2-chome Minato-ku.
Tel. 582-0111.
Indoor and outdoor pools; gymnasium and instructor.

IMPERIAL HOTEL, 1-1-1 Uchisaiwaicho, Chiyoda-ku.
Tel. 504-1111.
Pool; sauna; and massage room.

MIYAKO HOTEL TOKYO, 1-1-50 Shiroganedai, Minato-ku.
Tel. 447-3111. Separate gymnasium for men and women; indoor pool.

TOKYO HILTON INTERN. 6-2 Nishi-Shinjuku 6-chome, Shinjuku.
Tel. 344-5111. Tennis courts; indoor pool; gymnasium.

## Telephone & Telegraph Services

Public telephones are abundant and for tourists there is a special Travel Phone service with English speaking staff. **Dial**: 502 1461. Use a yellow, blue or green public phone (not red) and insert a 10 Yen coin which will be returned at the end of the call.

International Direct Dialling is available at all major hotels.

Public telephones come in four different colours and the calls are metered at 10 yen per three minutes. The colour coding of public phones (red, pink, yellow, and blue) designates where you will find them and the type of coinage that they will accept.

Red phones accept 10 yen coins only, six at a time, and are found outside shops. Store owners will take these phones in at closing time.

Pink phones are similar to the red phones, are privately owned and found inside shops and cafes.

Blue phones are found in telephone booths in public places. The wall mounted phones accept ten 10 yen coins and the shelf sitting phones accept six.

The yellow phones are useful for long distance calls as they accept 100 yen coins (ten 10 yen coins and nine 100 yen coins). These phones are also found in public booths.

## Tipping

In general it is not required that you should tip for services. Restaurants will automatically include a service charge, and taxi drivers won't expect any 'extras'. It is only at the more Western style places that you may find you have to provide a tip.

*Omote-Sando, Harajuku*

## TOURISM

Tourism is important to Japan, the country has been clever enough to reverse the normal trend of letting all the tourist dollar leave the country with the outbound tourist by ensuring much of it returns through tourism investment overseas.

As a tourist destination herself, Japan has much to offer in terms of culture, past traditions and a way of life that is unique. Accommodation, transport and sightseeing is well organised and up to world standards. However, Japan's strong *yen* has made the country an expensive country for those who are not prepared to work hard at looking for inexpensive accommodation, eating houses and public transport.

Coupled with cost is a tourism infrastructure that shows some glaring weaknesses which make it less than easy for the first-time visitor to get around.

For example, heavy traffic, a freeway system struggling to cope and insufficient English signs do not make Tokyo an easy city for those who would like to drive themselves.

In addition, the individual traveller who does not use a package tour with the preferential rates that apply, will find hotel rooms are costly and in-hotel services priced well above European and American averages.

The country also has a language problem. Although English is learnt by a majority of students the average tourist would be unaware of this as it is difficult for the English-speaking traveller to be understood outside hotels and information offices.

The rail system, the most heavily used of all transportation in Japan, is not geared for foreigners. Confusion and frustration inevitably arise in the crowded stations where there is a dreadful lack of English-language signs to explain routes, timetables and fares. Staff are of little value as ticket collectors and station attendants speak only Japanese.

But the careful tourist can have an inexpensive holiday through a little ingenuity in selecting small, local restaurants and braving the urban rail system, there are still many who are not psychologically equipped to cope with this type of vacation and are best advised to stick with the proven tourist packages.

The biggest trap for the unwary traveller is the night-life. Tokyo is notorious for its bars and nightclubs where the bill at the end of the evening can look like Mt. Fuji. Even by Japanese standards these clubs are expensive and rarely you will see anyone picking up the check unless on a company expense account.

All this can add up to a tourist nightmare but to balance it out you have a safe, clean city, people willing to help despite any language barrier, efficient and prompt services, a wide range of accommodation, excellent sightseeing and a charm on the part of local residents which is pleasantly surprising. However fore-warned is fore-armed and no intending visitor should be put off by the tales of woe you hear....just be aware of them, that's all.

## Tourist Services

Government Tourist offices:

**Australian Tourist Commission**, Sankaido Bldg., 9-13, Akasaka 1-chome, Minato-ku. Tel: 585-0705.
**Austrian National Tourist Office**, Palace Bldg., 1-1, Marunouchi 1-chome, Chiyoda-ku. Tel: 215-6791.
**Belgian National Tourist Office**, Tameike Tokyu Bldg., 1-14, Akasaka 1-chome, Minato-ku. Tel: 586-7041.
**British Tourist Authority**, Tokyo Club Bldg., 2-6, Kasumigaseki 3-chome, Chiyoda-ku. Tel: 581-3603.
**Canadian Govt. Travel Bureau**, Yamakatsu Bldg., 5-32, Akasaka 8-chome, Minato-ku. Tel: 479-5851.
**Danish National Tourist Office**, Sanno Grand Bldg., 14-2, Nagata-cho 2-chome, Chiyoda-ku. Tel: 580-8360.
**Finnish National Tourist Office**, Imperial Hotel, 1-1, Uchisaiwai-cho 1-chome, Chiyoda-ku. Tel: 504-0905.
**French Govt. Tourist Office**, Landic No.2 Akasaka Bldg., 10-9, Akasaka 2-chome, Minato-ku. Tel: 582-6965.
**German National Tourist Office**, German Bunka Kaikan, 5-56, Akasaka 7-chome, Minato-ku. Tel:586-5046.
**Govt. of India Tourist Officer**, Pearl Bldg., 9-18, Ginza 7-chome, Chuo-ku. Tel: 571-5062.
**Greek National Tourist Office**, No.11 Mori Bldg., 6-4, Toranomon 2-chome, Minato-ku. Tel:503-5001.
**Hawaiian Visitor's Bureau**, Shin Kokusai Bldg., 4-1, Marunouchi 3-chome, Chiyoda-ku. Tel: 287-2651.
**Hong Kong Tourist Association**, Toho Twin Tower Bldg., 5-2, Yuraku-cho 1-chome, Chiyoda-ku. Tel: 503-0731.
**Italian Govt. Tourist Organization**, Lions Bldg., 1-2, Moto Akasaka 1-chome, Minato-ku. Tel: 478-2051.
**Japan National Tourist Organization**, Tokyo Kotsu Kaikan 10-1, Yuraku-cho 2-chome, Chiyoda-ku. Tel: 216-1901.
**Korea Tourist Bureau**, Hosokawa Bldg., 1-16, Akasaka 1-chome, Minato-ku. Tel: 585-0400.
**Malaysia Tourist & Information Center**, Nichiginimai Kyodo Bldg., 3-4, Nihonbashi Hongo-cho, Chuo-ku. Tel: 279-3081.

**National & International Tourist Bureau of Indonesia**, 9-13, Akasaka 1-chome, Minato-ku. Tel: 585-3588.
**Netherlands National Tourist Office**, No. 10 Mori Bldg., 18-1, Toranomon 1-chome, Minato-ku. Tel: 508-8015.
**New Zealand Govt. Tourist Office**, 5-2, Yuraku-cho 1-chome, Chiyoda-ku. Tel: 508-9981.
**Representative for Singapore Tourist Promotion Board Japan**, Yurakucho Denki Bldg., Minamikan, 7-1, Yuraku-cho 1-chome, Chiyoda-ku. Tel: 287-1326.
**Sri Lanka Tourist Board**, 2-1, Atago 1-chome, Minato-ku. Tel: 432-7838.
**Spanish Govt. Travel Bureau**, Mori Bldg., 11-8, Nishi Azabu 1-chome, Minato-ku. Tel: 403-5991.
**Tourist Orginisation Of Thailand**, Hibiya Mitsui Bldg., 1-2, Yuraku-cho 1-chome, Chiyoda-ku. Tel: 580-6776.
**United States Travel Service**, Kokusai Bldg., 1-1, Marunouchi 3-chome, Chiyoda-ku. Tel: 212-2422.
**USSR Govt. Tourist Information Bureau**, Roppongi Heights, 1-16, Roppongi 4-chome, Minato-ku.
Tel: 584-6617.

## THE METRIC SYSTEM

### Length

| | |
|---|---|
| 1 millimetre | 0.04 inches |
| 1 centimetre | 0.39 inches |
| 1 metre | 1.09 yards |
| 1 kilometre | 0.62 mile |

Converting kilometres to miles is as simple as multiplying the number of kilometres by 0.62.(e.g. 10km's x 0.62 6.2 miles)

Converting miles to kilometres is done by multyplying the number of miles by 1.61 (e.g. 60mi x 1.61 96.6km's)

### Capacity

| | |
|---|---|
| 1 litre | 33.92 ounces |
| | 1.06 quart |

0.26 gallons

Converting litres to gallons, multiply the num'er of litres by .26. (e.g. 20l x .26 5.2 gallons)

Converting gallons to litres multiply number of gallons by 3.79. (e.g. 10 gal x 3.79 37.9l)

## Weight

1 gram 0.04 ounces
1 kilogram 2.2 pounds

Converting kilograms to pounds, multiply number of kilos by 2.2. (e.g. 55 kg x 2.2 121 pounds)

Converting pounds to kilograms, multiply number of pounds by .45. (e.g. 100 pounds x .45 45 kilos)

## Area

1 hectare 10000m/sqr or 2.47 acres

Converting hectares to acres, multiply the number of hectares by 2.47 (e.g. 10 ha x 2.47 24.7 acres)

Converting acres to hectares, multiply the number of acres by .41 (e.g. 40 acres x .41 16.4 ha)

## Temperature

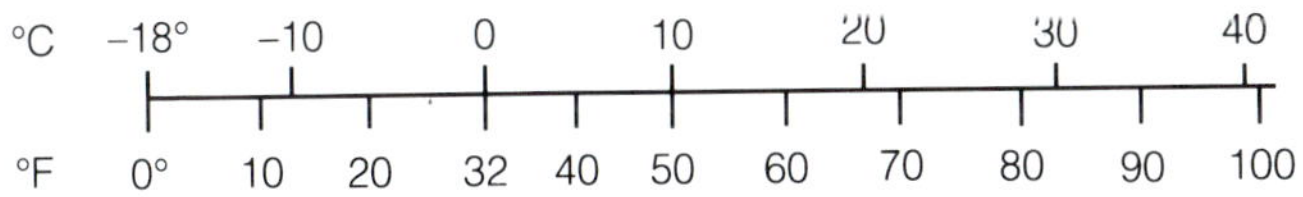

*Beer Hall, Ginza*

# PART V
## Business Guide

*Akasaka, Tokyo*

# BUSINESS GUIDE

Contents



## Business Briefing

**Main industries**: Steel, shipping, motor vehicles, chemicals, electronics, computers, scientific & optical.

**Main agricultural products**: Rice, barley, wheat, mandarin, oranges milk.

**Main imports**: Most raw materials, coal, cotton, wool, wheat, sugar.

**Principal trading partners**: United States, Korea, China, Germany, Australia, Hong Kong,Saudi Arabia.

> **INFOTIP**: Business people should always carry business cards. It is one of the first rituals you will undergo at a business appointment. The card not only provides your identity it also enables your opposite number to assess your ranking in the company.

## Import & Export of Currency

Foreign exchange regulations are being relaxed and there is little restriction on the importation of foreign currency. However there are limits to the amount of Japanese currency which can be exported. A local Japanese embassy, consul, trade commission or bank will advise on the current limitations.

## Banks

Foreign banks with their own offices or representative offices include:

| | |
|---|---|
| Bank of America, | Midland, |
| Chase Manhattan, | Bank of England, |
| Citibank, | Westpac, |
| American Express, | National Australia, |
| Hong Kong, | ANZ, |
| Deutsche, | Banque National de Paris, |
| Barclay's, | Credit Suisse. |

Major Japanese banks:

| | |
|---|---|
| Mitsubishi, | Bank of Japan, |
| Daiwa, | Bank of Tokyo, |
| Dai-ichi Kangyo, | Fuji, |
| Sanwa, | Kyowa, |
| Sumitomo, | Mitsui. |

**Bank hours:**
weekdays 9 a.m. -3 p.m. and Saturday 9 a.m.-12 noon.

## Currency Exchange & Banking

The Japanese currency is the yen. There are coins of the value 1, 5, 10, 50, 100 and 500, and notes of the value 500, 1000, 5000 and 10,000. All coins and banknotes are marked with arabic numerals. Foreign currencies will need to be changed into Japanese currency at an authorised money exhanger. Banks, because they offer a more favourable rate of exchange, are the best places to change currency. However if only small amounts are involved you may as well change at the cashier in your hotel or at a major store. It is not a bad idea to cash a small amount upon arrival at the airport or at your own bank before departure as this will give you some cash in hand for bus, taxi (if you particularly wealthy) or train fares into the city. For greater convenience it is possible to open cash card accounts at banks or savings accounts at post offices if staying for any length of time.

Bank hours: weekdays 9 a.m. -3 p.m. and Saturday 9 a.m.-12 noon.

> **INFOTIP:** In any business negotiation do not lose your temper with the Japanese. Not only do you look foolish and 'lose face' but it will have no effect and only force the 'victim' to become more intransigent.

## Chambers of Commerce & Trade Org.

All Japan International Traders Federatiion,
Dai-Ichi Bldg.,Asakusabashi 1-chome Tel.866 5941
American Chamber of Commerce,
Tosyo Bldg., 2 Maranouchi,3-chome Tel 211 5861
Association for Promotion of Intl.Trade,
Nihon Bldg., 6 One-machi 2-chome Tel. 270 3631
Australian Chamber of Commerce,
Imperial Hotel. Tel. 501-7031
British Chamber of Commerce,
World Import Mart,Ikebukuro 3-chome Tel. 987 1620
British Export Marketing Centre,
Pola Aoyama Bldg.,Minato-ku.Tel.402 6121
Japan External Trade Organisation,
Kyodo Tsushin Bldg, Minato-ku Tel. 582 5511
Japan Foreign Trade Council,
World Trade Centre, Minato-ku. Tel. 435 5952
Japan Overseas Development Corp,
Mori Bldg. Minato-ku Tel. 437 1911
Tokyo Foreign Trade Association,
Tokyo trade centre, Minato-ku. Tel. 435 5394
Unitod Statos Trade Centre,
World Import Mart Bldg., Toshima-ku Tel. 987 2441

## Business Publications in English

Mainichi Daily News.
Japan Times.
International Herald Tribune.
Tokyo Journal.
Japan Economic Journal.
Tokyo City Guide.
Time.
Newsweek.
South China Morning Post.
Far East Economic Review.
Asiaweek.

**INFOTIP:** Japan Airlines will prepare business cards for you with your name and company written in Japanese. This excellent service is worth taking advantage of.

## Guide Interpreter Services

For qualified and authorised guides and interpreters contact the Japan Guide Association on 213 2706.

## Parcel & Courier Services

A number of local companies as well as Japan Airlines offer freight and parcel services around the world. Courier services include the world-wide DHL and Federal Express companies.

**INFOTIP:** The Japanese like to both give and receive gifts. Take something peculiar from your country if possible when visiting Japan for business purposes.

## Social Clubs

Tokyo British Club,
Ebisu. Tel. 443 8092
Tokyo Toastmasters Club,
Tel.0474 47 0314
Willhouse International Club.
Tel. 380 8000
Tokyo Athletic Club,
Nakano-ku Tel.384 2131
Tokyo YMCA,
Chiyoda-ku Tel. 293 1921
Tokyo YWCA,
Chiyoda-ku Tel 293 5421

Rotary and Lions Clubs have several chapters. Major hotels have details of meeting times and places.

## Major Airlines

**Aeroflot Soviet Airlines, Tatsunuma Bldg., 3-19, Yaesu 1-chome, Chuo-ku. Tel: 272-5311.**
**Aerolineas Argentinas**, suite 630, Pacific Hotel, 13-3 TTakamawa 3-chome, Minato-ku. Tel: 445-4951.
**Air Canada**, New Akasaka Bldg., 2-3 Akasaka 3-chome, Minato-ku.
Tel: 585-4635.
**Air France**, Shin Aoyama Bldg., Nishi-kan 1-1, Minami Aoyama 1-chome, Minato-ku. Tel: 475-2211.
**Air India**, Hibiya Park Bldg., 8-1 Yuraku-cho 1-chome, Chiyoda-ku. Tel: 214-7631
**Air New Zealand**, Hibiya Park Bldg., 8-1, Yuraku-cho 1-chome, Chiyoda-ku. Tel: 213-0968.
**Alaska Airlines**, Ayoma Kyoda Bldg., 6-18 Kita Aoyama 3-chome, Minato-ku. Tel: 407-8386.
**Alitalia Airline**, Tokyo Club Bldg., 2-6 Kasumigaseki 3-chome, Chiyoda-ku. Tel: 580-2175.
**All Nippon Airways**, Kasumigaseki Bldg., 2-5, Kumigaseki 3-chome, Chiyoda-ku. Tel: 580-4711.
**Aloha Airlines**, Shin Yuraku-cho Bldg., 12-1, Yuraku-cho 1-chome, Chiyoda-ku. Tel: 216-5877.
**American Airlines**, Kokusai Bldg., 1-1, Marunouchi 1-chome, Chiyoda-ku. Tel: 212-0861.
**Ansett Airlines of Australia**, Shin Kokusai Bldg., 4-1, Marunouchi 3-chome, Chiyoda-ku. Tel: 2146876.
**Austrian Airlines**, Palace Bldg., 1 1, Marunouchi 1-chome, Chiyoda-ku. Tel: 213-1751.
**Bangladesh Biman**, Kasumigaseki Bldg., 2-5, Kasumigaseki 3-chome, Chiyoda-ku. Tel. 593-1252.
**British Airways**, Hibiya Park Bldg., 8-1, Yuraku-cho 1-chome, Chiyoda-ku. Tel: 214-7851
**Canadian Pacific Airlines**, Hibiya Park Bldg., 8-1, Yuraku-cho 1-chome, Chiyoda-ku. Tel: 212-5811.
**Cathay Pacific Airways Ltd**. 5-2, Yuraku-cho 1-chome, Chiyoda-ku. Tel: 504-1531.
**Egypt Air**, Palace Bldg., 1-1, Marunouchi 1-chome, Chiyoda-ku. Tel: 211-4521.
**Ethiopian Airlines s.c.**, Mori Bldg., 4-10 Nishi Shinbashi 1-chome, Minato-ku. Tel: 501-0782.
**Finn Air**, Imperial Hotel, 1-1, Uchisaiwai-cho 1-chome, Chiyoda-ku. Tel: 504-0905.
**Garuda Indonesian Airways**, Kasumigaseki Bldg., 2-5, Kasumigaseki 3-chome, Chiyada-ku. Tel: 593-1181.
**Hawaiian Airlines**, Shin Kokusai Bldg., 4-1, Marunouchi 3-chome, Chiyoda-ku. Tel: 214-4774.
**Iran Air**, Akasaka Habitation Bldg., 3-5, Akasaka 1-chome, Minato-ku. Tel: 586-2101.

**Iraqi Airways**, Akasaka Matsudaira Bldg., 4-1, Akasaka 3-chome, Minato-ku. Tel: 586-5801.

**Japan Air lines**, Head Office: 7-3, Marunouchi 2-chome, Chiyoda-ku. Tel: 284-2666.

**Jat Yugoslav Airlines**, Bunzan Bldg., 31-6, Shinbashi 4-chome, Minato-ku. Tel: 434-3843.

**Kenya Airways**, Yurakucho Bldg., 10-1, Yuraku-cho 1-chome, Chiyoda-ku. Tel: 214-4595.

**KLM Royal Dutch Airlines**, Yurakucho Denki Bldg., 7-1, Yuraku-cho 1-chome, Chiyoda-ku. Tel: 216-0761.

**Korean Air lines**, Shin Kokusai Bldg., 4-1, Marunouchi 3-chome, Chiyodaku. Tel: 211-3361.

**Lufthansa German Airlines**, Tokyo Club Bldg., 2-6, Kasumigaseki 3-chome, Chiyoda-ku. Tel: 580-2121.

**Malaysian Air System**, Hankyu Kotsusha Bldg., 3-9, Shinbashi 3-chome, Minayo-ku. Tel: 503-5961.

**Mexican Airlines**, Sanno Grand Bldg., 14-2, Nagatacho 2-chome, Chiyoda-ku. Tel: 593-2573.

**Olympic Airways**, Air France Bldg., 5-5, Akasaka 2-chome, minato-ku. Tel: 583-6854.

**Pakistan International Airwlines**, Yurakucho Bldg., 10-1, Yuraku-cho 1-chome, Chiyoda-ku. Tel: 216-4641.

**Pan American World Airways**, Kokusai Bldg., 1-1, Marunouchi 3-chome, Chiyoda-ku. Tel: 240-8888.

**Philippine Airlines**, Sanno Grand Bldg., 14-2, Nagata-cho 2-chome, Chiyoda-ku. Tel: 580-1571.

**QANTAS Airways**, Tokyo Chamber of Commerce Bldg., 2-2, Marunouchi 3-chome, Chiyoda-ku. Tel: 211-4481.

**Sabena Belgian World Airlines**, Address Bldg., 2-19, Akasaka 2-chome, Minato-ku. Tel: 585-6551.

**Scandinavian Airlines**, Toho Twin Tower Bldg., 5-2, Yuraku-cho 1-chome, Chiyoda-ku. Tel: 503-8181.

**Singapore Airlines**, Yurakucho Bldg., 10-1, Yuraku-cho 1-chome, Chiyoda-ku. Tel: 212-1011.

**Thai Airways International**, Toho Twin Tower Bldg., 5-2, Yuraku-cho 1-chome, Chiyoda-ku. Tel: 503-8181.

**Trans Australia Airlines**, Shin-Yurakucho Bldg., 12-1, Yuraku-cho 1-chome, Chiyoda-ku. Tel: 216-5828.

**Trans Mediterranean Airways**, CBC Int'l Bldg., 22-7, Shiba 3-chome, Minato-ku. Tel: 454-2561.

**Trans World Airlines**, Hibiya Park Bldg., 8-1, Yuraku-cho 1-chome, Chiyoda-ku. Tel: 212-8876.

**United Airlines**, Kokusai Bldg., 1-1, Marunouchi 3-chome, Chiyoda-ku. Tel: 213-4511.

**UTA French Airlines**, Kasumigaseki Bldg., 2-5, Kasumigaseki 3-chome, Chiyoda-ku. Tel: 593-0771.

**Varig Brazilian Airlines**, Palace Bldg., 1-1, Marunouchi 1-chome, Chiyoda-ku. Tel: 211-6761.

**Western Airlines**, Kokusai Bldg., 1-1, Marunouchi 3-chome, Chiyoda-ku. Tel: 213-2777.

*Omote-Sando, Tokyo*

LEGEND
Main Road
Railway
International Airport
Airport
0
100
200
Kilometres
CHINA
Vladivostok
North Korea
Seoul
YELLOW SEA
South Korea
Oki-Shotō
Matsue
Himej
Strait
Korea
Tsushima
Yamaguchi
Shimonoseki
Takamatsu
Kita-Kyūshū
Matsuyama
Chejudo
Fukouka
Kochi
Kurume
Ōita
SHIKOKU
Gotō-retto
Nagasaki
Yatsushiro
KYŪSHŪ
Miyazaki
Kagoshima

USSR
USSR
Wakkanai
Abashiri
Kitami
HOKKAIDŌ
Asahikawa
Sapporo
Obihiro
Kushiro
Tomakomai
Muroran
Samani
Hakodate
Aomori
Hirosaki
Hachinohe
SEA
OF
JAPAN
Akita
Morioka
JAPAN
Yamagata
Sendai
Sado-Shima
HONSHU
Kōriyama
Nagaoka
Utsunomiya
Hitachi
Toyama
Komatsu
Matsumoto
Tsuchiura
TOKYO
Kofu
Ogaki
Kawasaki
Yokohama
Fuji-san
Biwa-ko
Nagoya
Yokkaichi
Kobe
Osaka
OCEAN
PACIFIC

*West District, Shinjuki*

朝日生命

## Alphabetical Index

Notes

Notes